In the Garden at Max Gate.

THOMAS HARDY'S WESSEX

BY

HERMANN LEA

ILLUSTRATED FROM PHOTOGRAPHS
BY THE AUTHOR

TOUCAN PRESS, (J. STEVENS COX)
MOUNT DURAND, ST. PETER PORT.
GUERNSEY C.I.

© J. Stevens Cox, 1966

1st Ed. MacMillan and Co., Ltd., 1913
2nd Ed. 1925
3rd Ed. Toucan Press, 1969.

CONTENTS

PART I

NOVELS OF CHARACTER AND ENVIRONMENT

CHAPTER I

CHAPTER II

CHAPTER III

CHAPTER IV

CHAPTER V

PART II

ROMANCES AND FANTASIES

CONTENTS

CHAPTER IV

PART III

NOVELS OF INGENUITY

CHAPTER I

PART IV

POETICAL WORKS

CHAPTER I

ILLUSTRATIONS

ILLUSTRATIONS

THE WESSEX OF THOMAS HARDY

ILLUSTRATIONS

ILLUSTRATIONS

INTRODUCTION

THE object of this book, as its title indicates, is to depict the Wessex country of Thomas Hardy, with a view to discovering the real places which served as bases for the descriptions of scenery and backgrounds given us in the novels and poems. But before commencing our survey I should like to direct attention to certain facts which it seems necessary to grasp for the proper understanding of such discoveries as we shall presently make.

To begin, we will take a general glance at the tract of country covered by our author. There has been an impression current amongst some people that Thomas Hardy's Wessex is limited to the county of Dorset, but we have it on his own assurance that the Wessex of the novels and poems is practically identical with the Wessex of history, and includes the counties of Berkshire, Wilts, Somerset, Hampshire, Dorset, and Devon—either wholly or in part. We are told in the preface to " A Pair of Blue Eyes " that " the shore and country about ' Castle Boterel ' (approximately Boscastle) is the farthest westward of all those convenient corners wherein I have ventured to erect my theatre . . . and it lies near to, or no great way beyond, the vague border of the Wessex kingdom." The author's ingenious disinterment of the old name leads us to consider for a moment the actual boundaries of this former kingdom. They can only be guessed at. According to the Saxon Chronicle, the kingdom was

founded by the Prince Cerdic and Cynric his son, who
landed in the year 494, and who, after some successful
battles against the Welsh, became kings in 519. We
have only conjecture to go upon, but it seems probable
that southern Hampshire and the Isle of Wight
were the earliest locations. Whether Cerdic—a
name probably of Welsh origin—actually founded
the kingdom of Wessex must remain a matter for
debate. But wherever it was founded, and by whom-
soever, we have a certain amount of testimony to
prove that its boundaries were considerably expanded
during the reign of Ceawlin (560 to 592), and in 571
Aylesbury and the upper part of the Thames Valley
were conquered by the West Saxons; and again,
in 577, Cirencester, Bath, and Gloucester likewise
succumbed. A large portion of Somerset was annexed
by Cenwalh (643 to 672), and by the end of the
seventh century the rest of that county and certain
parts of Devonshire were added. The area now
reached is that usually shown on maps, and roughly
corresponds with that adopted by our author. During
the reign of Ecgberht (808 to 836) Sussex, Surrey,
Kent, and Essex became an integral portion of
Wessex. Then followed an interval during which
there were further annexations, certain divisions, some
reunions, until in 871 the whole kingdom passed to
Alfred, except such parts as were under Danish rule.

In 878 a peace was established between Alfred of
Wessex and the Danes, by which it was agreed that
the boundary line should be regarded as the Thames,
northward up the Lea to its source, thence to Bedford,
and along the Ouse to Watling Street—the old Roman
road from London to Chester. By this treaty, London,
Middlesex, and part of Hertford, became an absolute
part of Wessex. During the years of comparative
peace which ensued, Alfred inaugurated the first
attempts at defensive warfare, as well as a restoration
of the schools. Later he was engaged in active
warfare with the Danes, and when he died in 900 he

INTRODUCTION

left the kingdom of Wessex still unconquered. From that time, Edward the Elder, his son, worked hard in subduing the Danes and absorbing them among his own subjects until the year 918, when the last of the Danish Kings of East Anglia was slain, and that realm annexed. Then followed many vicissitudes, ending in the Norman Conquest.

It is now more than twenty years since I first became interested in tracing the topographical features of the Wessex Novels, and as I have lived in Wessex continuously during that period, and have travelled

THE BIRTHPLACE OF MR. THOMAS HARDY.

over practically all the main roads, and many of the lanes and by-roads—traversing more than 150,000 miles on a cycle, in a car, on foot—I have had peculiar opportunities for following out my hobby. In 1904 I wrote a small guide-book to such portions of the scenery as came within the boundary of Dorset; but this was in no sense exhaustive, and dealt only with some of the principal backgrounds. For the purposes of the present book I have revisited every one of the spots described.

My attention has frequently been drawn to in-exactitudes or misstatements that have appeared in the many guide-books to the Wessex country which have already been published. These have very likely arisen through a desire on the part of the writer to make the fictitious places conform to the real in an absolute, dogmatic manner. Should any such inaccuracies have crept into the present book I must ask my readers' kindly indulgence. I have not read any of the published guide-books, fearing lest I might be led into a form of plagiarism which would be distasteful. References have been made to certain county histories and other recognised works of authority, but the bulk of the descriptions have been written on the actual spots visited.

To those who desire to follow an itinerary with detailed exactitude I would suggest reference to the one-inch ordnance maps of the district. These furnish all necessary information as to roads, lanes, paths, woodlands, and hills.

In the text of the Wessex Novels are many dialectic words, phrases, and idioms, most of which may still be heard occasionally in the remoter districts. Probably, as William Barnes held, the speech of Dorset and the adjoining counties was the outcome of the Anglo-Saxon language rather than a mere dialect, nearly all of the words being traceable to their origin. The *New Oxford Dictionary* includes a number of these dialectic expressions which have been supplied by the author of the Wessex volumes.

The task of writing this book has been a very pleasant one, providing many interesting experiences ; and my thanks are due to those who have aided me, either by giving information or by permitting me to photograph their houses. To more than any one else I am indebted to Mr. Hardy himself for correcting me in a few identifications of some of the places which, owing to the meagre clues in the text, defied discovery by any other means.

In regard to the more intimate details which we are setting out to elucidate, it may be said first that with the characters themselves I have, of course, nothing to do. This may appear an unnecessary observation, till I mention that more than one curious inquirer has asked me whether such-or-such a character in one of the stories is not intended to be a portrait of X——, and has then given the name of a person living in or near the place which the fictitious name is supposed to represent. Next, the houses, churches, and other architectural features which are to claim

MAX GATE—THE RESIDENCE OF MR. THOMAS HARDY.

our attention are plainly not each depicted from one real model—for some are undoubtedly composite structures. In some cases there are distinct clues from which we may draw our deductions : described peculiarities in the fabric of a building ; the interchange of place and character names ; the construction of the name itself, relating to some obvious characteristic of a town or village. The natural configurations, such as the hills, heaths, downs, and woods, are, for the most part, so faithfully pictured that we may venture to be almost dogmatic in reconciling them with their counterparts, while many of them appear under their established names.

Nevertheless, I want to make it very clear at the outset that the descriptions given in the novels and poems must be regarded in their totality as those of imaginative places. The exact Wessex of the books exists nowhere outside them, as Mr. Hardy himself indeed has hinted. Thus, instead of declaring *Casterbridge* to *be* Dorchester, we dare only say that the presentment is undoubtedly founded on salient traits in the real town. Certain stages, certain scenery and backgrounds, are essential to the setting of every drama, but it has been left for Thomas Hardy to describe such accessories in a manner that probably no other writer, before or since, has ever accomplished. This fact it is which makes our work both easier and at the same time more interesting. The realistic treatment which the setting of the stories receives creates rather a dangerous position for the topographer, since there is an undoubted tendency to fall into the error of confusing the ideal with the actual.

Should any disappointment arise in the minds of those who visit the existing places—on account of any want of similarity between these and the book descriptions—he may be reminded, in addition, that most of the stories were written many years ago, and that, in the interval which has now elapsed, Time and the hand of man have been responsible for many alterations, and have brought about actual obliterations of what were close originals at the date of portrayal. When the Wessex writer first turned his attention to verse and fiction he can have had no conception of the prominence to which he would attain among living authors—nor could he have anticipated the searching nature of the investigations that would be made into the scenery which served him as pattern.

There is another point to which I should like to draw attention, and that is the strange manner in which the scenery adapts itself to, and identifies itself with, the characters themselves. We have a striking instance of this in the life-history of Tess. Her child-character develops at *Marlott* (Marnhull), an unsophisticated village somewhat isolated from the outside world, remote from any large town, and where she is little prepared to cope with a man of the world such as Alec d'Urberville. It is in the sombre shades of Cranborne Chase, dark with its primeval yews and oaks, that her betrayal is effected. It is in the Froom Valley, within sight and sound of the crystal streams, where the grass grows lush and the air is fragrant with the scents of many flowers—the whole scene typical of growth—that we find the creation and expansion and maturing of that all-absorbing love which was to remain with her throughout her life. It is at *Wellbridge* that her repulse by Clare and her realisation of the full bitterness of life comes to her— that ancient home of her ancestors, a place filled with associations of a mouldy past, the home of those gruesome portraits, where the very atmosphere seems to be charged with things sinister. The phase of her hopelessness finds her at *Flintcomb-Ash*, a spot cursed by sterility, where Nature looks with an unkindly eye, and blesses not the labour of man's hand. When in utter despair she becomes callous and joins d'Urberville, it is at *Sandborne* we find her—that place of "fashionable promenades and new villas." And at last, when the officers of the law demand her as a victim to the merciless Mosaic recrimination dictated by a lust for revenge, the scene is Stonehenge, where the ancient Druids, the representatives of a god whose anger and love of destruction could only be appeased by the shedding of innocent blood, had sacrificed their thousands. We have only touched on a few instances, but the other scenes are equally appropriate.

H. L.

PART I

NOVELS OF CHARACTER AND ENVIRONMENT

CHAPTER I

THIS being the most widely read of the Wessex Novels, it is convenient to place it first in the examination of their scenery and backgrounds. The action takes place over a wide stretch of country—from Salisbury Plain in the north to Dorchester in the south ; from the New Forest in the east to Beaminster in the west. In leading my readers over the ground covered by the different scenes, and in pointing out certain towns, villages, houses, and natural landmarks, it must be clearly understood—as I have already shown in the Introduction—that these are merely originals which approximate to the imaginative backgrounds set up by our author. In the volume with which we are now dealing such features have been rendered more realistically than in some others, and accordingly we find little difficulty in reconciling the actual with the ideal.

The story opens by introducing us to John Durbeyfield as he journeys homewards to *Marlott* from *Shaston*, and the meeting with Parson Tringham, "the antiquary of Stagfoot Lane (Hartfoot Lane)," which reveals to him that the name of Durbeyfield is synonymous with d'Urberville — obviously a close imitation of the real name of a family now extinct in the county.

We will precede Durbeyfield and enter the village of *Marlott* (Marnhull, more or less). It "lay amid

3

the north-eastern undulations of the beautiful Vale of Blakemoor or Blackmoor . . . in which the fields are never brown and the springs never dry" (1). The "Forest of the White Hart" is an alternative name for the valley which our author occasionally employs. Marnhull would seem to be a corruption of its original name of Marlhill, a more significant title, referring apparently to the white clay or marl which crops up there and which, after exposure to the air, hardens into a freestone. The church and many of the houses are built of it. Marnhull was once quite a considerable place; the remains of many streets may be traced where the houses have entirely disappeared. The dwellings now are curiously disconnected, many wide gaps intervening, but new buildings are rapidly springing up, and the village bids fair to assume its old size at no very distant date. Its old notoriety for drunkenness and general debauchery has now passed away, and it is no longer known as "the booziest place in Dorset."

Here we meet Tess for the first time, "in her right hand a peeled willow wand, and in her left a bunch of white flowers," making her way with the other village maidens to the field where the May-dance was to take place. Towards them came Durbeyfield, driving in a vehicle belonging to the *Pure Drop* Inn (2). This inn figures many times in the book, and may, by its position in the village, be recognised as "The Crown." *Rolliver's*, the other inn mentioned, would seem to be suggestive of the "Blackmoor Vale Inn," on the western and lower side of the straggling village.

The only other feature with which we have to deal at the moment is the old cottage in which Tess was imagined to have been born, but this, alas, appears to have been swept away. From the description of its situation we may assume that it stood at the end of the village nearest to Shaftesbury. At this village, too, Angel Clare comes on the stage;

1.—THE BLACKMOOR VALE.

2.—MARNHULL.

and we are made acquainted with Mrs. Durbeyfield and the younger children.

The next background in Tess's history with which we are concerned is exhibited when she starts for *Casterbridge* (Dorchester) very early in the morning to deliver the load of bee-hives. After passing the little town of *Stourcastle* (approximately Sturminster Newton) the road rises steadily towards Hazelbury Bryan—a village we shall visit later. *Stourcastle* is never more to us than a halting-place, though there is some historical interest attaching to it.

A hamlet near by was the birthplace of William Barnes, the Dorset poet, a statue of whom stands in the church close of St. Peter's at Dorchester. Sturminster Newton was the home of Robert Young, "An olde Dorset Songster," whose poems, written under the pseudonym of "Rabin Hill," have lately been collected and published in a small volume. Just outside the town, on the other side of the river Stour, is a mound, the site of a castle where King Alfred is said to have lived. Near by is a picturesque old mill, one of the few of its kind remaining in Wessex (3).

A few miles beyond *Stourcastle* Tess and Abraham came in sight of Bulbarrow, rising high on their left hand. This camp has a circular, double entrenchment, generally supposed to be of Celtic origin. It is the second highest point in Dorset. From its summit extends on all sides a magnificent view, the eyes of the beholder penetrating far over Dorset into the adjoining counties. Many places interesting to Hardy readers can be identified from here with the aid of a glass, and amongst others is "the hill-town called Shaston."

It is to this place that Tess walks when she goes to visit her reputed relative; and from here she rides in the carrier's van which travelled to *Chaseborough* and passed near *Trantridge* (suggesting Pentridge)— "the parish in which the vague and mysterious Mrs. d'Urberville had her residence." *Shaston* enters largely

3.—THE MILL, STURMINSTER NEWTON.

4.—PENTRIDGE CHURCH.

into the book entitled "Jude the Obscure," and our only present interest in it is when, on her return journey, Tess slept the night "at the house of a cottage woman they knew." The actual cottage is not further indicated and we must leave its position unidentified. If we approach the town towards evening from the direction of Cranborne we shall see it just as our author describes it, "standing majestically on its height; its windows shining like lamps in the evening sun."

The house to which Tess was journeying, known in the story as *The Slopes*, was situated near the little village of *Trantridge* on the borders of Cranborne Chase (4). We may regard this house as purely imaginary, or at least as having been drawn from a model in some other district, for there is no house here answering to the description, though there is one near Wimborne. This village also figures in one of "Life's Little Ironies." It lies about three miles from Cranborne and is close to the Wiltshire boundary. Its name is derived from the British word Pen, meaning a head or the principal part, and hence the apex of a hill; close to it is Penbury Hill, where a beacon once stood.

The next place presented is when Tess goes with the other work-people to spend a Saturday evening at *Chaseborough* (nearly Cranborne), and stands late at night waiting for them to start homewards. Cranborne is the market town of the district; it was famous both in Saxon and Norman times for its monastery; the church now in existence is one of the oldest and largest in the county of Dorset. It is partly Norman, partly Early English, with some later Perpendicular work, and contains many interesting tablets and monuments. The curfew is rung every night except on Sunday, and following it the date of the month is tolled. The fine Tudor manor-house which stands near the church takes the place of a building which was one of the favourite resorts of King John; some of the internal walls may possibly be of that king's date. The name Cranborne is supposedly derived

8

from Anglo-Saxon words denoting "crane" and "river"—the winding of the river here suggesting somewhat the neck of a crane. Previous to the construction of the Western Turnpike the high road from London to the west led directly through the town. It is still an excellent road, and is praised as such in

5.—THE "FLEUR-DE-LIS," CRANBORNE.

"Barbara," in "A Group of Noble Dames," of which anon. The only feature of the town which particularly interests the Hardy student is the *Flower-de-Luce* Inn, where Alec d'Urberville discovered Tess waiting for her companions. Its prototype, the "Fleur-de-Lis," is readily discovered, the name being often now, and formerly always, pronounced as spelt in the novel (5).

We are now brought to the environment of the first real tragedy in Tess's career—when she found herself at the mercy of Alec d'Urberville. *The Chase* (Cranborne Chase) was a chase proper, and must not be confused with a forest—a prerogative of kingly right. It embraces an area of some 800,000 acres and is "the oldest wood in England." One may readily wander for mile after mile in this ancient Chase without meeting a single human being; and although certain tracts have been brought under cultivation, there is a tendency for these to revert again to forest. No fitter scene could have been chosen for such an episode.

6.—A TYPICAL TEXT.

Subsequently we follow Tess back to *Marlott*, when she meets the text-writer—an individual who is by no means extinct at the present day. On many a gate and stile in the Wessex lanes and by-ways we may discover evidences of his industry in quotations more or less apt, but nearly all of gloomy, Calvinistic significance (6). Once again in her old home, we find her sensitive nature seeking refuge in the bedroom which she shared with some of the other children. We see the fields wherein she worked by day, and the hill-sides and the woods to which she wandered by night. It is here, at *Marlott*, that her baby is born, and here that it dies and is buried "in that shabby corner of God's allotment where He lets the nettles grow." There is no stone to mark the place of burial, and as the churchyard to-day is scrupulously neat and well cared for, its appearance at the date of the story can only be imagined. Down to the third quarter of the last century, however, such corners were often reserved in country churchyards for that reprobate class of person designated.

Our next scene is at the dairy at *Talbothays*, the location of which has evoked considerable controversy amongst those who have attempted to identify the places mentioned in the Wessex Novels. It may be stated definitely that the dairy-house is drawn from no particular building, but that it is typical of many of the dairies which occur in the Froom Valley. We are informed that it lay in "The Valley of the Great Dairies, the valley in which milk and butter grew to rankness . . . the verdant plain so well watered by the river Var or Froom" (7). From the summit of a hill only a short distance from *Weatherbury* (largely Puddletown as it formerly was) Tess first saw her future place of sojourn. The picture before her was a complete contrast to the one she had gazed upon from childhood : there everything was of smaller proportions — smaller fields, smaller herds of cows ; here were vast stretches of water-meads, huge herds of cows. The peculiar difference in the atmosphere is also strikingly noticeable : the Valley of the Froom, watered by the swiftly flowing river, is lighter, clearer, altogether more brilliant in appearance than the Blackmoor Vale, which always seems to strike the traveller afresh with a certain sense of oppressive heaviness, the stiffer nature of the soil adding to the feeling.

The description in the novel of the position occupied by the dairy in relation to other landmarks would seem to indicate that, in the writer's fancy, the spot lay at no great distance from the junction of the Dorchester-Tincleton and Puddletown-Ilsington roads, on the southern margin of *Egdon Heath*, and in full view of Rainbarrows—a section of country which will have our further attention when we treat of "The Dynasts" and "The Return of the Native." This location of *Talbothays* is sufficiently indicative to enable us to follow Tess in thought as she goes about her various duties at the dairy; or when, in her hours of leisure, she wanders with Angel Clare "along the meads by creeping paths which followed the brinks of trickling tributary brooks." It may be mentioned that "Talbots" or "Talbothays" ("hays" means hedges) is the real name of a small freehold estate in the neighbourhood that was owned by our author's father at the time the story was written, and is still in the possession of a member of his family; but at that date there was no house standing upon it, nor was ever a dairy there, then or since; so that the name only was borrowed.

The Froom Valley sweeps through Dorset from above Maiden Newton, till the river empties itself into the tidal estuary at Wareham, and contains the most fertile and valuable land of its kind in the country; the carefully tended irrigated meadows producing an abnormal amount of grass forage and supporting huge herds of cows (8). Many months, full-charged with happenings, passed over Tess during her stay in the Froom Valley—"that green trough of sappiness and humidity," and here we see the intimacy between her and Angel Clare passing from mere acquaintance to friendship, and from friendship to marriage. The latter's position in regard to the other dairymaids and the subsequent effect on their natures is also brought out here. The episode of Clare carrying the four girls through the water instances this point. They were on their way to the service at *Mellstock* (Stinsford) church, and he overtook them just as they reached that part of the road which was flooded with water. A portion of the road near Bockhampton Bridge lies very low and is often flooded in winter, so that we may be within reason in

7.—WATER MEADOWS IN THE FROOM VALLEY.

8.—THE RIVER FROOM.

surmising that it was here the occurrence is supposed to have taken place.

West Stafford Church would seem to represent the place at which Tess and Clare were married. It is in its reality a building containing some interesting Jacobean woodwork (9). They had decided to spend the early days of their union at one of the ancestral homes of the d'Urbervilles. The way there is now, as then, along a level road that follows the river more or less closely until it nears the village of Wool. Then, turning to the left and passing " over the great Elizabethan bridge," we come upon *Wellbridge House* (Wool-Bridge House), clearly seen from the train as it enters the station of Wool (10). It is probable that, of all the scenes which occur throughout the Wessex Novels, no place is so near to reality or so familiar to my readers as this house. Inside it may be found the old mural portraits which had such an effect on Tess's imagination. Up to the time at which the novel was published they were quite distinct, but since then injudicious washing with soap to make them clearer has resulted in their being nearly obliterated altogether, though we can still trace the gruesomeness attributed to them. Interest of a psychical nature intrudes here, for I have it on the best of evidence that this weird effect actually does make itself felt on certain temperaments, people having told me of the ghastly dreams that have come to them after viewing these portraits. Another similar peculiarity attached to Wool-Bridge House is the legend of the coach. Clare had spoken of it, but had refrained from telling the whole story, and it is not until near the end of her life that Tess hears it fully, from the lips of Alec d'Urberville. According to local superstitions, it is said that the d'Urberville coach passes over the bridge hard by and draws up at the old house on Christmas Eve, but that the sound of its transit is only audible to the ears of certain individuals ; also that it presages death or some dire calamity. I have known more

9.—West Stafford Church.

10.—Wool-Bridge House.

than one local character declare that the house was haunted; though an old lady who lived there for some time practically alone told me she had never heard nor seen anything that could be regarded as preternatural. This evidence, however, counts for very little, only certain natures seeming to be gifted with the power of sensing psychic phenomena.

Soon after their entrance into the old house came to them the news of Retty Priddle's attempted suicide in the *Great Pool*. This we may well suppose to have been the same pool of which we have mention in "The Return of the Native," where it receives the name of *Shadwater Weir*.

Now comes before us the gloomy scenery of the second great tragedy in the life of Tess—the result of her confession of her past. This background is the Abbey of Bindon (11). We can easily follow Clare when, after entering Tess's room, lifting her from the bed, and bearing her downstairs and into the open air, he went along the river-side until they were opposite the mill, and, crossing the plank "which, lying a few inches above the speeding current, formed a giddy pathway for even steady heads . . . he reached the other side with her in safety . . ." and so gained "the ruined choir of the Abbey-Church." The empty stone coffin of the abbot, close to the north wall, in which Clare laid Tess is still there, and may be readily discovered, tourists sometimes giving themselves the grim pleasure of lying in it as Tess was made to do (12). The Abbey was of the Cistercian order and was founded in 1172, and though now entirely in ruins, as the novel states, it still possesses an impressive interest. The old fish-ponds, arched in by avenues of deciduous trees (13); the level grassed walks, once trodden by hordes of monks; the calm stillness which pervades the whole place; the half-obliterated foundations, marking the once extensive walls which enclosed cloister, guest-house, refectory, kitchen, hospitium, sacristy and dormitories, together with the many other

11.—BINDON ABBEY.

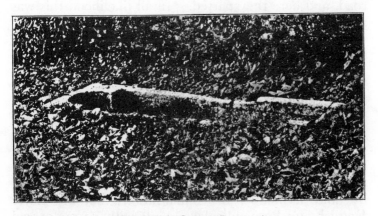

12.—THE ABBOT'S COFFIN, BINDON ABBEY.

offices pertaining to the Abbey—all tend to lead the mind into speculative channels of thought on the conditions of life when the Abbey was in its prime, and the changes wrought by time which it must have witnessed.

The mill, which stands just outside the Abbey enclosure and is going busily at this hour, interests us as that at which Angel Clare is supposed to have worked for a time to gain experience of the business (14). We are told in the novel that it had "in centuries past been attached to the monastic establishment. The mill still worked on, food being a perennial necessity; the Abbey had perished, creeds being transient."

We now come to the places connected with the exit from *Wellbridge* and the separation of Clare and Tess. After calling on the Cricks at *Talbothays*, they drove together through *Weatherbury* and *Stagfoot Lane* (Hartfoot Lane) until they reached the village of *Nuzzlebury*, or *Nuttlebury* (suggestive of Hazelbury Bryan), on the outskirts of the Blackmoor Vale. Some miles beyond this village they came to a cross-road, and here they parted. In all likelihood this was just outside the little town of Sturminster Newton. Leaving Clare for the present, we will follow Tess as she drives onwards through the familiar Blackmoor Vale until she reaches the entrance to *Marlott*. Thence on foot she approaches her father's house by a back lane.

Meanwhile, Clare is pursuing his way westwards towards *Emminster* (Beaminster). This is our first visit to the place clearly indicated as "the hill-surrounded little town" with "the Tudor church-tower of red stone" (15). Beaminster has been devastated by quite a number of conflagrations, but the Early English and Perpendicular church with its sculptured tower has always escaped undamaged. William Barnes gives us the following description of the town:

13.—THE OLD FISH-PONDS, BINDON ABBEY.

14.—BINDON MILL.

> Sweet Be'mi'ster, that bist a-bound
> By green an' woody hills all round,
> Wi' hedges, reachen up between
> A thousan' vields o' zummer green,
> Where elems' lofty heads do drow
> Their sheädes vor haÿ-meakers below,
> An' wild hedge-flow'rs do charm the souls
> O' maidens in their evenen strolls.

There is a curious custom still in vogue at Beaminster : on Sundays it is usual for many of the inhabitants to lock their doors when going to church and to leave the keys in the locks outside! The origin of this proceeding is obscure, but it may have arisen from the fact that some of the keys were ponderously heavy. Clare did not stay here long, but soon left the country for Brazil.

The next place to notice is a dairy near *Port-Bredy* (approximately Bridport). Of the exact location we have no knowledge, but we read it was situated "equally remote from her native place and from Talbothays." This is where Tess lives after her new departure from *Marlott*, but when work becomes difficult to obtain she decides to join Marian on "an upland farm in the centre of the county," and presently we see her starting to walk thither. "She reached *Chalk-Newton* (adumbrating Maiden Newton), and breakfasted at an inn." We shall visit Maiden Newton later when we are examining the country suggested by the descriptions in the short story entitled "Interlopers at the Knap," and it will suffice now to notice that little old hostel called the Castle Inn, standing close beside the river (16). Then Tess trudged on, until she drew near to Marian's place of sojourn—*Flintcomb-Ash*.

The actual position of *Flintcomb-Ash* has always been a debatable point with explorers in the Hardy country. To begin with, the farm-house cannot be pointed out, though such farm-houses do exist in the vicinity. But the actual site which served our author

15.—BEAMINSTER CHURCH.

16.—THE CASTLE INN, MAIDEN NEWTON.

for his description is discoverable. If we will ascend the steep hill-side by a track leading out of Alton Pancras village to the eastward we shall soon reach a flat plateau. It is known locally as Barcombe Down. If we now follow along the crest of the hill we shall in due course light upon the ridged turf which marks the site of what was once a British village. For what reason the ancient people of Britain should have selected so bleak and unproductive a spot as this it is hard to determine. Marian described it as a "starve-acre" place—a title which is truthfully descriptive to-day. Vast numbers of flints lie uncovered on the chalky surface, making walking no easy matter, while the wind which sweeps over the plain greets the traveller with an unsympathetic touch. There is a sardonic aspect in the landscape, and the scene which stretches before us is all in harmony with the sufferings that Tess endured there.

It was after she had been at *Flintcomb-Ash* some little while that she determined to call at *Emminster* parsonage for tidings of Clare (17). The road she took was a rugged one, but quite practicable; a glance at the ordnance map will enable us to trace it exactly. From near the British Village a track-way descends by Church Hill to the high road; here we shall see a serpentine lane—Barn Lane—ascending the steep hill due westward. At its junction with the Sherborne-Dorchester road we must turn northwards for a little way, when we shall find another lane leading to the left. If we follow its windings, and cross the Sherborne-Cerne road at the point called Lyon's Gate, still making westward, we shall pass over High-Stoy and come in due course to the stone pillar Cross-in-Hand, or Crossy Hand as it is called locally. This is a walk which many people have taken since the publication of the story, and it will reward the pedestrian with a beautiful and varied prospect, the woodland that lies below to the northward including practically the whole of the background which serves for the novel entitled

17.—BEAMINSTER VICARAGE.

18.—THE COTTAGE BY THE CHURCH, EVERSHOT.

"The Woodlanders"—the country of *The Hintocks*. The diversity of landscape from right hand to left hand is truly amazing ; the utter loneliness, the almost oppressive silence of Nature, add a weird touch which is intensified by coming suddenly upon this solitary landmark, Cross-in-Hand, springing up from the grassy down like the stem of a giant mushroom.

This stone pillar forms the *motif* of the poem entitled "The Lost Pyx," and under the chapter on "Poems of the Past and the Present" I shall have occasion to refer to it further. Just now it stands before us as being the stone whereon Tess placed her hand when, at Alec d'Urberville's demand, she swore never to tempt him. The occurrence, it will be remembered, took place on her return walk, d'Urberville coming thus far with her, and, after the oath had been registered, leaving her side to plunge into the valley in the direction of *Abbot's-Cernel* (Cerne Abbas). "Of all spots on the bleak and desolate upland this was the most forlorn," says our author—an estimate which I can endorse from personal observation ; and I can also corroborate his finding "something sinister, or solemn, according to mood, in the scene amid which it stands."

Continuing her journey towards Clare's home, she would come in the course of three miles to another high road, called Long Ash Lane ; crossing this, she would soon reach the village of *Evershead* (apparently Evershot). The "cottage by the church" at which she halted and breakfasted is obvious enough to the passer-by to-day(18). Benvill Lane, the real name of the second half of her route, leads up to "the edge of the basin in which Emminster and its Vicarage lay," where her resolution died and she fruitlessly retraced her steps.

The barn in which Alec d'Urberville, now "a excellent firey Christian man," was preaching was most probably drawn from the barn which stands near the centre of the village of Evershot and was originally used as a chapel. Tess heard him preaching as she passed through the village on her return walk (19). Still

24

is also to be seen, beyond the northern part of Long Ash Lane, "the road ascending whitely to the upland along which the remainder of her journey lay."

A fresh landscape is led up to by Tess's route to the home of her childhood, where she goes on learning of the illness of her parents. A walk to Marnhull in the darkness from the place we have considered to be *Flintcomb-Ash* is no easy matter: fifteen miles of ascent and descent till Bulbarrow is mounted, and then a plunge down into the heavy-scented Blackmoor Vale. At *Nuttlebury* (Hazelbury Bryan) the village inn—bearing the sign of " The Antelope," we may remark—is passed as she passed it, and we trace "the maze of lanes she threaded" and re-enter Marnhull.

After the disasters that succeed one another here we follow her with all the family on a migration to *Kingsbere*. The loading of the waggon with their household goods and their journey along the road describes a scene which can be witnessed in Dorset any year on the 6th of April (Lady Day, old style), when the work-people move from farm to farm; the miscellaneous collection of goods useful and goods ornamental, with babies of various ages wedged in between pieces of furniture, as though to keep the latter from shifting about, is quite a common sight, and the emigrants often form veritable processions along the roads and lanes. Turning " the flank of an eminence which formed part of the upland called Greenhill"—scene of the fair in " Far from the Madding Crowd "—we dog them to the " half-dead townlet "—as our author designates Bere Regis—where their ancestors reposed in the vaults beneath the church.

Kingsbere (Bere Regis), as its name indicates, was once a royal residence, and is supposed to have contained a palace belonging to Queen Elfrida; it was likewise a Roman station. The church is a fine building of flint and stone, chiefly Perpendicular in style, but with some Norman work in the interior; it was fairly well restored by G. E. Street many years ago (20).

19.—THE ROAD TOWARDS CROSS-IN-HAND, EVERSHOT.

20.—BERE REGIS CHURCH.

It contains three canopied tombs in Purbeck marble, as also a traceried window with heraldic emblems pertaining to the Turberville family (21). This obviously suggested the window of the novel under which the bedstead was erected. In the parish register may be seen the original signature of " Tho. Turberville," dated " May ye 10th 1679." The vaults of this family lie under the adjacent aisle, with an inscription on the entrance-stone, as mentioned in the book. They are now sealed up, but till lately people were living who had descended into them and had seen the coffins of generations of the name.

Clare's return to England, his short sojourn at *Emminster* Vicarage, and his search for Tess in the last phase of her life-history, gives us another lead through the landscapes. We may follow him as he leaves his father's house and proceeds along Benvill Lane, passes the *King's Hintock* (Melbury Osmund) estates, and the solitary pillar Cross-in-Hand, till he reaches *Flintcomb-Ash*, and thence goes to *Marlott* —localities we have already examined. We track him to *Shaston*, and to the little village in which he was informed the Durbeyfield family had settled, where he learns that Tess is at *Sandbourne* (Bournemouth). We duly follow him thither.

The description of this watering-place, with " its piers, its groves of pines, its promenades, and its covered gardens . . . like a fairy place suddenly created by the stroke of a wand, and allowed to get a little dusty," is well known, and is almost literal. The lodging-house called " The Herons," where Clare finds Tess, and where the great tragedy of the book is assumed to occur, it is impossible and undesirable to distinguish.

It is difficult to trace their flight—there being, of course, no tangible track of a pair " avoiding high-roads, and following obscure paths tending more or less northward . . . into the depths of the New Forest." They are said to have reached the empty

21.—The Turberville Window, Bere Regis Church.

22.—Moyle's Court.

28

house known as *Bramhurst Manor-house.* There are many such houses in the environs of Ringwood, but a careful examination persuades me that the mansion bears a strong resemblance, both in construction, furniture, and surroundings, to Moyle's Court—once the residence of Dame Alice Lisle, from which she was taken by the myrmidons of Jeffreys to her execution at Winchester. The house, by the way, is said to be still haunted by her spirit (22).

Their course northwards from here merges into clearness as they approach "the steepled city of *Melchester*" (approximately Salisbury). *Melchester* bulks more largely in "Jude the Obscure" and other of the Wessex Novels than in the present one, so that we need not pause to contemplate it now. "The graceful pile of cathedral architecture rose dimly on their left hand;"[1] they passed quickly through the city, and were soon following the road which led them to Salisbury Plain. They were now close to Stonehenge, the mysterious pagan temple, the greatest sight of its kind in the country (23). In the chronicles of Nennius (ninth century), the date of its origin is placed in the fifth century A.D.; but according to other and later writers it is supposed to have been erected one hundred years before Christ. Readers will not need to be reminded that there has been much controversy regarding its date and its origin; no authentic proofs are forthcoming to establish any of the various contentions.

Here they are imagined to have waited till the morning dawned and Tess's pursuers came upon them and led her away towards *Wintoncester* (Winchester). This favoured city, which preserves much of its old-time historic interest, and over which the hand of the vandal has passed lightly, forms the last background we have to inspect. If we climb upon one of the hills close to the town we can verify the description given by our author (24). It still lies "amidst its convex and

---

[1] It should be noted that, owing to a mistake in the printing, this has, in most editions, appeared as the *right* hand.

23.—STONEHENGE.

24.—WINCHESTER.

concave downlands"; there before us is the "sloping High Street," the "West Gateway," the "mediæval cross," and "the bridge." We can go to-day to the top of the West Hill and find the milestone beside which Angel Clare stood with Liza-Lu, waiting "in paralysed suspense" for the final signal. But trees have grown up in later years, and it is not possible to obtain from that point now the view that was obtainable at the time of the novel—except in portions—but an approxi-

25.—WINCHESTER GAOL.

mate view can be seen from another point, a little to the westward, of "the broad cathedral tower," and the other particular features described in the text (25).

For the same reason one cannot behold from the milestone—at least, one could not when the present writer was there—the "large red-brick building, with level grey roofs, and rows of short, barred windows bespeaking captivity" in which "justice was done, and the President of the Immortals (in Æschylean phrase) had ended his sport with Tess." Perhaps Nature's screening is well.

CHAPTER II

"FAR FROM THE MADDING CROWD"

MOST of the action in this book takes place in and around the farmstead fictitiously called *Weatherbury Farm*; but before we proceed to that place we will examine the backgrounds which form the setting for the earlier scenes. Our first introduction to Gabriel Oak and Bathsheba Everdene is on the apex of *Norcombe Hill*. We take this to represent Toller Down, where the road to Crewkerne from Dorchester passes through a cutting. It is a spot which figures also in the poems entitled "A Tramp-woman's Tragedy" and "The Home-coming," where its natural characteristic of loneliness, tinged with an air of desolation, are further exemplified. "It was a featureless convexity of chalk and soil," we read,—this hill whereon stood Oak's farm—"half-wooded, half-naked . . . covered on its northern side by an ancient and decaying plantation of beeches." Standing 800 feet above the sea, Toller Down lies exposed to the full force of the Atlantic gales, hard to struggle against in autumn and winter when the prevailing wind is westerly.

Our interest soon changes to *Casterbridge*, which we cannot doubt to be drawn in the likeness of Dorchester. It is the date of "the yearly statute or hiring fair," and in imagination we can see the street wherein stand "from two to three hundred blithe and hearty labourers waiting upon Chance." This fair is still held, but year by year it loses its

32

26.—PUDDLETOWN VILLAGE.

27.—WATERSON HOUSE.

importance, and to-day is little more than a mere gathering of pleasure-seekers, interspersed with a few persons intent on business. We shall probably search in vain for the carter with his emblematic piece of whipcord in his hat; or the thatcher with his "fragment of woven straw"; though the shepherd with his inevitable sheep-crook may be noted occasionally.

We may journey in company with Oak as he walks towards *Shottsford*—an imitation of the town of Blandford. Leaving Dorchester by the London Road, he passes the "water-meadows traversed by little brooks," and at three miles reaches *Yalbury Wood* (Yellowham Wood), ascends the hill of *Yalbury*, and later on comes to *Weatherbury* village (26). It is then that he notices the fire, and strikes across country to *Weatherbury Farm*. The model which served our author may be found in Waterson House; though to fulfil its purpose in the story we must imagine it placed nearer to Puddletown village — for it was Puddletown, in its old guise of fifty or more years ago, which suggested the *Weatherbury* of the Wessex Novels. To be quite exact, however, and to bring the farm and the village into proper focus, we must cut out a section of the country which intervenes between them, to the extent. perhaps, of a mile, or rather more.

Waterson House has suffered from a fire since the date of the story, destroying all the old woodwork; it has moreover passed into other hands quite recently, and extensive alterations are in progress. Nevertheless, we may still trace many of the features described in the book before us. To Oak it showed itself as "a hoary building, of the Jacobean stage of Classic Renaissance"; and we still find the "fluted pilasters" that graced its front, together with the "soft brown mosses, like faded velveteen," patched on its roof (27).

Little Weatherbury Farm, the imaginary home of Boldwood, was probably drawn from Druce farm-

28.—DRUCE FARM.

29.—CHINE HILL.

house, which stands a full mile nearer Puddletown (28). A short distance from it is the little cluster of cottages known as Chine Hill, amongst which we notice an old whitewashed house with a thatched roof suggesting *Nest Cottage*, the place where Oak lived after his dismissal from Bathsheba's employment (29). In the meadow facing this cottage we may find the "sheep-washing pool . . . a perfectly circular basin of brick-work" which served as a theatre for one of the scenes (30). But the "Great Barn," in which the sheep-shearing was supposed to take place, we shall search for hereabouts in vain. Its "vast porches . . . dusky, filmed, chestnut roof . . ." have either all been swept away, or those features have been imported into the story from a neighbouring place, there being two or three barns in South Dorset of which this would be a faithful description—Cerne Abbas in particular.

We will now turn our attention to *Weatherbury* village. Alas, domestic Puddletown to-day also exhibits little of its old-time characteristics; the site of Warren's Malthouse is now occupied by a neat park fence and shrubbery—and so with most of the other features. Any one entering the well - kept village to-day would grasp little idea of its ancient importance as a small market town. We have it recorded that about the year 1860 Puddletown "contained as many as twenty bootmakers, twelve blacksmiths, twenty carpenters and wheelwrights, five pairs of sawyers, two coopers, and some cabinet-makers."[1]

The church, which figures so frequently in the narrative, stands near the square, where in the old days stood the stocks and the court-house (converted later into a private school). This church was one of the finest, interiorly, of any in the county of Dorset, but its recent (1911) alterations, demolitions, and additions have been looked on with dismay by many archæologists, the late Perpendicular chancel having been converted into a much more spacious new one (31).

[1] From *Memorials of Old Dorset*.

30.—THE SHEEP-WASH, DRUCE.

31.—PUDDLETOWN CHURCH.

The "little gallery door," through which Troy was supposed to have entered the church, may be seen on the west side of the tower (32); and we can likewise see the porch in which he is said to have passed the night (33). The gargoyle, described as "too human to be called a dragon, too impish to be like a man, too animal to be like a fiend, and not enough like a bird to be called a griffin," has been imported from another parish. The huge old elm trees which stood within the churchyard have been felled recently—another matter for regret to those who regard ancient features with respect.

In Troytown, a handful of houses lying at the bottom of *Yalbury Hill*, we recognise "the road-side hamlet called Roy-town." It was once a place of Celtic occupancy, and we may still trace the remains of a miz-maze, or labyrinth, where ancient spectacles were produced. The inn known to us as the *Buck's Head*, the place where Joseph Poorgrass halted with the body of Fanny Robin, was pulled down a few years ago, though it had ceased to be an inn before its demolition (34).

Several times in the course of the story we are interested in *Casterbridge*. The Corn Exchange was a "low though extensive hall, supported by beams and pillars." If we enter the present building on a market day we shall be struck with the similitude of its human scenes now to what they are described as being then. Here are the farmers with their sample bags of corn, pouring out the contents into their hands—just as we read of Bathsheba doing. We shall, however, look in vain for "the town-bred fowls" who used as a matter of fact to frequent the building in order to pick up the scattered grains.

"The bridge over the Froom"—Grey's Bridge—figures in this story, as well as in so many other of the novels and poems. We see Fanny Robin pausing here to rest on her way to the Union. The other, poorer bridge, at the bottom of the town—Swan

32.—The Gallery, Puddletown Church.

33.—The South Porch, Puddletown Church.

34.—INTERIOR OF THE BUCK'S HEAD INN, TROYTOWN.

35.—LULWORTH COVE.

36.—WOODBURY HILL.

37.—THE SHEEP FAIR, WOODBURY HILL.

Bridge—is where, also in our mind's eye, we see Troy awaiting Fanny and, failing her arrival, journeying to *Budmouth* (approximately Weymouth) to attend the races.

At the "White Hart Tavern," still standing at the lower end of the town, Troy meets Pennyways. The gaol comes before us when Boldwood goes there to give himself up after shooting Troy. This was, of course, the old building, and must not be taken as identical with the present county gaol.

Yalbury Hill (Yellowham Hill) has been briefly alluded to; it bulks more prominently in "Under the Greenwood Tree" and other of the series; but there are certain references to it in the present volume. As Bathsheba and Troy are slowly driving up the hill from *Casterbridge* Market they meet Fanny, at that hour on her way to the Union Workhouse. Over this hill passes Boldwood as he walks to the gaol.

With *Sherton Abbas*—the imaginatively treated Sherborne—we have little to do here, save that the turnpike house which still stands at the top of the hill leading down into the town marks the spot where Oak and Coggan overtake Bathsheba when she is on her way to Bath to meet Troy.

Bath, according to Cainy Ball, possessed "great glass windows to the shops, and great clouds in the sky, full of rain, and old wooden trees in the country round." Bathsheba was married here, also Lady Constantine in "Two on a Tower"—of which anon.

Lulworth Cove—in the phraseology of our author *Lulstead* or *Lulwind Cove*—is a background for one short scene (35). Troy reaches this wonderful little basin shut in by rocks the day following his visit to Fanny's grave, and goes out for a swim. We read of his being caught in the current and carried out from the shore. "Far in the distance Budmouth lay upon the sea."

A fresh background comes before us when Bathsheba goes to the fair at *Greenhill* (36). If we visit

38.—The Pleasure Fair, Woodbury Hill.

39.—The Main Thoroughfare, Woodbury Hill.

Woodbury Hill, close to Bere Regis, on September the 21st, we shall receive an excellent impression of the "Nijni Novgorod of South Wessex." The site marks an ancient British, or Belgic-British, Camp. The fair is said to have been started by a certain packman who, while passing near the hill, was caught in a thunderstorm which drenched him and soaked his pack. After the storm had passed over he climbed to the summit of the hill and spread his cloths and woollens to dry. Some of the villagers from Bere Regis chanced to see the waving cloths and went up out of curiosity, with the result that they promptly purchased all the stock. On that same day in subsequent years the packman again sought the hill-top, having found it such a first-rate market-place; his conduct was followed by other vendors; and in course of time an annual fair grew out of the chance visit (37). When at its zenith the fair lasted for three weeks, but as markets became more common it gradually declined into a short week, and finally to two days. Once huge flocks of sheep and many cattle and horses changed hands, but to-day there is very little actual business done, and it is little more than a gathering of mere pleasure-seekers (38). The first day of the fair used to be known as "gentlefolks' day"; the last as "pack-and-penny day" (39). It is here we see Troy again after his temporary exit from the stage; Bathsheba, Boldwood, and many other of our friends are also present; and while on the road homewards Bathsheba is supposed to give Boldwood her conditional promise to marry him.

We should like to find the cottage in which Oak is said to have lived, and where Bathsheba comes to him, but, like so many other cottages of that date, it has disappeared completely.

CHAPTER III

"JUDE THE OBSCURE"

THE tract of country which we shall now examine is in the northern portion of Wessex, and as we endeavour to trace the footsteps of Jude from *Marygreen* to *Christminster*, and then to *Melchester* and *Shaston*, and ultimately back to the last scenes of his life at *Christminster*, we shall come upon many spots which only concern us in this one story. Since it was the last written of the Wessex Novels we shall naturally expect to find the various towns that form models for the backgrounds less altered than is the case in some of the earlier stories, and this expectation will not be disappointed. The striking similitude which we shall note as existing between the places described to us in the book and the real places which we shall visit makes us very liable to err, and to declare that this or that fictitious place is actually the place we are examining. The feeling is even more strongly forced upon us when trying to elucidate the scenery connected with Jude's history than with any other volume of the series, and so accentuated is the impression that when we come upon the grass-patch at *Marygreen* (40), five miles south from Wantage, it would require very little imagination to think of the characters as real people who had actually lived and had their being there. In fact, we may find ourselves saying, "Here is the place, but where is Jude?"

To examine the arenas of action as they succeed each

other in chronological sequence : The story opens at *Marygreen*, and if we would find the spot which seems to answer to the description given we must go to the downland of southern Berkshire, where by dint of much climbing up and across the hills we shall at length come to the quiet village of Great Fawley, set deeply amidst the undulations of a sparsely populated district, where the cultured land has been wrested from the wild at great pains on the part of the reclaimers. The name of the place at once arrests our attention as providing Jude with his surname, a plan of our author's which is by no means unusual with him.

In July the downs are gay with their carpeting of flowers ; the roads which bisect the huge tract of grass-land are white, glaringly white in the sunlight, and the impalpable pallid dust of the chalky soil rises freely at the slightest hint of a breeze. Great Fawley is great only in comparison to its lesser neighbour Little Fawley, for in itself it is but a hamlet. If we make our way to the upper part of the village we soon step upon the Green. Near its margin is an old well (41) ; here is a school-house ; there stands the church ; and yonder is a cottage. We have to pull ourselves up smartly, or we shall be declaring positively that *Marygreen* is before our eyes, instead of only the place it symbolises. From the Green we can catch a glimpse of the *Brown House*—known locally as the Red House—with the long stretch of cultivated land sloping up to it (42).

It is here, at *Marygreen*, that Jude is supposed to have passed the early years of his life, in toil that jarred on his sensitive nature and in circumstances that handicapped him at every turn in his struggle to attain to his ideal, to reach *Christminster*, that city of perfection where the tree of knowledge flourished —far to the northward beyond the hills that encompassed the village and shut it in from the outside world. In imagination we see Jude taking his first step towards his emancipation when he climbs the

40.—THE GREEN, GREAT FAWLEY.

41.—THE WELL, GREAT FAWLEY.

hill until he reaches the high road at its junction with the old ridgeway, "the Icknield Street and original Roman Road through the district." The old trackway, now entirely grass-grown, is still plainly visible, stretching across the downs until it seems to merge into them and lose its identity. Reaching this spot, Jude was close to the *Brown House*, and by mounting a ladder which stood against it he was able to see in the sky to the northward the halo of light which hung over *Christminster*—virtually Oxford. The high road running eastward still forms the dividing line which separates the cultivated arable land from the natural downland, just as it did when Jude's history was being unfolded to us.

A wide and magnificent view is before us on every hand at the summit of the hill, and a point which cannot fail to strike the beholder is its aloofness from sophistication, and the untrammelled nature of all the surroundings. Surely the environment is aptly chosen, for it would be in just such natural conditions that we should expect a highly-strung and somewhat romantic nature like that of Jude to develop along the lines described, imbibing strange, perhaps weird, ideas regarding life ; the commonplace things of every day assuming proportions greater than they really bore. There is much ancient history shut up within these hills, leading the most prosaic mind to speculate on the peoples of a bygone age who moved amongst them and had their being in the midst of these Berkshire wildernesses.

Alfredston (potentially Wantage) now claims our attention, for it was here that Jude went for a time as apprentice to a stone-cutter. To students of the Wessex country Wantage is interesting as being the birthplace of King Alfred in 849, for to him is due much of the credit of making Wessex what it is. In the centre of the market-place stands a large statue to his memory (43). The origin of its fictitious name becomes clear to us when we realise the connection

42.—The Red House Barn.

43.—Wantage.

of the place with the old Wessex ruler. Other than the town itself as a whole there is little detail to claim us, and we soon turn our steps towards *Cresscombe*.

A clue is given to its position in regard to Wantage and Great Fawley, and when our search takes us to the little village of Letcombe Bassett we quickly realise its close approximation to the *Cresscombe* of the story. It is a rough track thither from Great Fawley and difficult to find, but the village is easily reached from Wantage by the direct road. After we strike the river and follow beside it for a short while we come upon a picturesque thatched cottage standing right among the watercress beds (44); and again we see the appositeness of its coined name. The cottage seems somehow familiar to us, and it does not require much stretch of fancy to picture Arabella and her happy-go-lucky parents as its once inhabitants, so good a model is it for our author's description. Here, at *Cresscombe*, was the first and odd meeting of Jude and Arabella, a meeting destined to colour the whole of his future life.

Before we leave this vicinity to discover the next back-scene we shall naturally wish to find that "lonely roadside cottage between the Brown House and Marygreen," where Jude lived after his marriage. But here we meet with disappointment; real as it has been and as it is remembered—starved fir-trees and all—it was completely destroyed by fire some twenty years ago, and only the site on which it stood can now be pointed out by the local residents.

If we follow in Jude's wake we shall come to *Christminster* in about fifteen miles (45). A greater contrast than that offered between the calm isolation of *Marygreen* and the thronged streets of *Christminster* it would be hard to imagine. We see Jude making his way thither with hope beating strongly in his heart. " He now paused at the top of a crooked and gentle declivity, and obtained his first near view of the city. Grey-stoned and dun-roofed, it stood within

44.—COTTAGE AT LETCOMBE BASSETT.

45.—MAGDALEN BRIDGE, OXFORD.

hail of the Wessex border." The action proceeds here for a considerable time; it is at *Christminster*, the city of his dreams, that Jude learns some of the bitterest lessons of life. Of the fact that Oxford provided our author with an outline from which was painted *Christminster* we can have but little doubt; many of the individual features mentioned are recognisable at a glance, and we need have no compunction in claiming the correlation.

It was at four o'clock one morning, when the streets were entirely deserted, that the present writer started to explore the city with a view of identifying the real with the artificial—a time of day eminently suited to the purpose. Perhaps High Street may seem familiar to us as *Chief Street*; Merton Street, with its cobbled paving, as the equivalent of *Old Time Street*; Carfax is undeniably the begetter of *Four Ways*; Christ Church brings *Cardinal College* to our minds; while Corpus Christi, or New, is substantially *Sarcophagus*. There can be no doubt that the Church of St. Mary-the-Virgin is identical with "the Church with the Italian Porch" (46); nor need we hesitate to discern in the Sheldonian Theatre, "the circular theatre with that well-known lantern above it," one of Wren's masterpieces, and more or less suggested by the ancient theatre of Marcellus at Rome.

With these features before us we shall find little difficulty in following Jude and the other characters as they move across the stage at *Christminster*. To attempt any adequate description of the town and its architecture would occupy far more space than need be allotted here; all such particulars can be gleaned from the various histories and guides readily obtainable. Here Jude first met Sue—at the ominous spot in Broad Street where the Martyrs were burnt. The cross in the pavement marks it still.

Shortly after we first became interested in *Christminster* we renew acquaintance with Phillotson in the school-house at *Lumsdon*. If we go to the village of

46.—Porch of St. Mary-the-Virgin, Oxford.

47.—The School-House, Cumnor.

Cumnor we shall find the original school-house from which Phillotson's residence was more or less drawn (47). No specially important episodes take place here, and our attention is soon diverted to an examination of that city of which the counterfeit name is *Melchester*.

We have already decided in a former chapter that, for the purposes of our idle wandering, Salisbury may be taken to represent *Melchester*. It would be easy to write volumes on the history of this ancient city, but it must suffice us now to examine only such individual features as occur in the story. It is here that Sue is supposed to come when she joins the "Melchester Normal School." The building which suggested the school is still a training college, and stands just outside the Close facing the western end of the Cathedral (48). The back of the house gives ready access to the river by passing down the length of the garden. "It was an ancient edifice of the fifteenth century, once a palace, now a training school, with mullioned and transomed windows, and a courtyard in front shut in from the road by a wall" thus our author. And if we choose to compare his description with the original we shall find it exact, saving in one or two minor details. The wall is now represented by iron railings, and the courtyard has been transformed into a lawn. The old building is honoured with the ghost of the murdered Duke of Buckingham a cause of creepiness at nights to the threescore young women in training there.

Very soon after Sue's arrival Jude takes up his quarters in the town, where he is said to have quickly obtained the work on which he had set his heart "the Cathedral repairs." (The building was restored by Sir Gilbert Scott between 1870 and 1880, and many workmen employed.) *Melchester* Cathedral, "the most graceful architectural pile in England," figures in several of the Wessex Novels, but is too well known to need any elaborate description here (49). It will be referred to again in a later chapter. Besides the

48.—THE TRAINING COLLEGE, SALISBURY.

49.—SALISBURY CATHEDRAL.

Cathedral and its Close, our attention is further claimed by the North Gate leading into High Street (50); the Market-house, and the "Grey Perpendicular Church with a low-pitched roof—the Church of St. Thomas"— in which Sue's marriage with Phillotson is supposed to have taken place. These, figuring under their real names, are easily studied (51).

From whichever direction we approach Salisbury, the spire of the Cathedral—the highest in the country —forces itself upon our view long before we become aware of human habitations. The town carries within itself an old-world atmosphere which is strongly intensified on market days by the presence of the country people who flock in from the surrounding villages, and by the snatches of dialect which break forth on all sides as we pass through the thronged market-square.

We are led to regard it as a day of much importance when Jude and Sue spend their holiday in visiting Wardour Castle—figuring under its rightful name. To the archæologist the somewhat severe Corinthian building is less interesting than the old castle near, surrounded by its magnificent trees, but now in utter ruin. The chief interest in the more modern building lies in its picture-galleries, well known to most lovers of art, and marked by the preponderance of the Italian School. We cannot locate definitely the cottage in which the weetless pair are said to have stayed the night, though we may surmise that it lay near Chicklade Ridge or Chilmark Down, in the direction of Wylye Station, from which place or Cadford they had intended to take train.

The *Kennetbridge* of the story suggests Newbury (52). Here lived the composer of the hymn that so haunted Jude; his journey thither, and the sense of disappointment with the man which it brought, forms an incisive episode in Jude's career. With *Kennetbridge* we shall have more to do anon.

The action now shifts to *Shaston* (typical of Shaftes-

50.—NORTH GATE, SALISBURY.

51.—THE CHURCH OF ST. THOMAS, SALISBURY.

bury). " The ancient British Palladour . . . was, and is, in itself the city of a dream," says our author. If we compare the description given in the book with the effect which is produced on us by a ramble through the town, we shall be struck with the exactness of his delineation. There is, of course, to-day the incongruous blending of the old and the new, but under the veneer of modern transmutations consequent on a spirit of commercialism we can still appreciate its ancient historic interests. " Vague imaginings of its castle, its three mints, its magnificent apsidal Abbey, the chief glory of South Wessex, its twelve churches, its shrines, chantries, hospitals . . .— all now ruthlessly swept away—throw the visitor, even against his will, into a pensive melancholy. . . ." Yes, *Shaston*—a historic contraction of Shaftesbury, by the way—to-day shows us but the skeleton of what it was in the Middle Ages, and there is a spirit of iconoclasm still at work which must, alas, result in further degradation to the ancient features of the old town (53).

Its position, raised high above the encompassing Blackmoor Vale, gives it an imposing appearance, and from it extends a superb view into the adjoining counties. From whatever direction the wind may blow, it smites the town with a vigour that threatens to sweep it from off its pedestal. " It was to this breezy and whimsical spot that Jude ascended " when he came to visit Sue, now Mrs. Phillotson, at the school-house. They lived in the house known as Old-Grove or " Old Grove's-Place," still to be seen standing almost opposite the school (54). The building dates back to the early part of the sixteenth century, and contains some interesting wood-carving. The " Abbey Walk " passes in front of the school, and leads towards the walls that face south. Of the Abbey itself, attached to what was perhaps the wealthiest nunnery in the country, nothing remains except the ruins of the walls which enclosed it, although the foundations of the Abbey Church and other relics are to be seen.

52.—NEWBURY.

53.—SHAFTESBURY.

Other features which receive cursory notice are the Duke's Arms Hotel in the Market Place, Bimport Street, and "the venerable graveyard of Trinity Church, with its avenues of limes," presented under their actual names.

Although there are traces of British and Roman occupation in the immediate neighbourhood, Shaftesbury has no history anterior to Saxon times, when it was a place of considerable importance. Legendary accounts connect the town with the date of King Solomon. Together with Dorchester, Bridport, and Wareham, it formed one of the four royal boroughs of Dorset. The industries carried on in the town in the seventeenth century—the manufactures of leather, worsteds, and buttons—have now completely died out.

For a brief space our characters are back at *Marygreen*, where we read of Jude's alienation from orthodoxy and the burning of his once treasured possessions: "Jeremy Taylor, Butler, Doddridge, Paley, Newman and the rest had gone to ashes."

This alteration in his principles comes almost concomitantly with that in Sue's, which now leads her to entreat Phillotson to sanction her leaving him and joining Jude. As the direct result of this request we picture him going to *Leddenton* to confer with his friend Gillingham. "Leaving Duncliffe Hill on the left . . . he crossed a tributary of the Stour, and reached Leddenton." It would seem to accord with the little town of Gillingham, washed by the river Leddon, or Loddon, the friend's name giving us a further clue to the identity of the place. To this townlet there is no other interest attaching.

It seems impossible to conjure up any spark of romanticism in regard to that eminently commercial town Reading. Yet it is an old town, and it is there that we must turn in order to follow the queer pair. *Aldbrickham* was doubtless drawn from Reading. It is essentially a place of progress, of constant alterations, whereby most of its ancient interests have become

54.—OLD GROVE'S-PLACE, SHAFTESBURY.

55.—THE GEORGE HOTEL, READING.

entirely shrouded by the present up-to-dateness. We find it impossible to locate the house in which Jude and Sue lived so long, and where he carried on his work as a monumental mason. There are hundreds of such houses in such streets. The George Hotel is easily discovered, however (55).

Stoke-Barehills—symbolising Basingstoke—is our next platform. It is an ancient place, and was once in occupation by the Romans, but here, too, we find with regret extensive alterations. Our author says of it : " It stands with its gaunt, unattractive, ancient church, and its new red-brick suburb, amid the open chalk-soiled cornlands. The most familiar object in Stoke-Barehills nowadays is its cemetery, standing among some picturesque mediæval ruins beside the railway. . . ." The mediæval ruins referred to are all that remains of the chapel of the Holy Ghost. It was founded in 1525, but in less than a century it lost its renown. Jude is supposed to have taken Sue and the boy to Basingstoke to see the agricultural show, when they were recognised by Arabella and her husband.

There is no distinctive name given to the church at which Jude and Sue were working as decorators, and the only guide we have to its position is the indication that it lay some two miles out of the town and at no great distance from the village of *Gaymead*. This village, as well as the town of *Aldbrickham*, comes before us again in the story entitled " The Son's Veto " —one of "Life's Little Ironics," and there we identify it as the fictitious presentment of Shinfield, a village lying a few miles to the south of Reading. Jude's discharge from his work at this church marks the declination of their fortunes, and from that time there commenced for them a " shifting, almost nomadic, life." Their wandering from place to place in search of work lasted for two years and a half, when we read of him " shaping the mullions of a country mansion, sometimes setting the parapet of a town-hall, some-

56.—THE SCHOOL-HOUSE, GREAT FAWLEY.

57.—GREAT FAWLEY CHURCH.

times ashlaring an hotel at Sandbourne (Bournemouth), sometimes a museum at Casterbridge (Dorchester), sometimes as far down as Exonbury (Exeter), sometimes at Stoke-Barehills (Basingstoke). Later still he was at Kennetbridge (Newbury). . . ." It is at this last place that Arabella comes again on the stage, and finds Sue selling cakes at a stall in the fair.

Our interest now reverts to *Christminster*. Here, in the temporary lodging, that gruesome scene—the hanging of the children by the boy, Father Time—is supposed to have been enacted. "Done because we are too menny" was the pencilled line he left behind to explain his action. Following closely on this tragedy we learn of the great change which is working in the minds of our two principal characters. Jude's outlook on life now becomes heterodox; Sue's paganism merges into orthodoxy, leading her to enter frequently the church of *St. Silas* for meditation or prayer.

This church was said to be situated in the most populous district of the city, termed *Beersheba*. This gives us a clue to its whereabouts, and a little search shows to us that *Beersheba* is probably a pseudonym of "Jericho," while the church of *St. Silas* is in the likeness of St. Barnabas (designed, by the way, by the late Sir Arthur Blomfield, R.A., with whom our author studied Architecture).

Phillotson is now back at his old school-house at *Marygreen*, and in order to rejoin him Sue goes thither—by train to *Alfredston*, driving near to the village, and walking the remainder of the distance. "She crossed by the well and under the trees to the pretty new school on the other side" (56). The following morning sees them re-married in the new church which stands but a short distance from the school-house (57).

Immediately following this event we are told of Jude's reunion with Arabella. She discovers him in the tavern whereat she was once a barmaid (a place we cannot locate definitely), and aids in making him drunk. Then we see her leading him towards her

58.—QUEEN'S COLLEGE, OXFORD.

59.—THE SHELDONIAN THEATRE, OXFORD.

65

father's house, passing the Martyr's Cross in Broad Street.

Jude's health now becomes worse. We may track him as he journeys by rail to *Alfredston* and walks the five miles to *Marygreen*. Here he has an interview with Sue in the church, and then we watch him as he retraces his steps, leaving behind him the old familiar footpath which led across "the fields in which he had scared rooks as a boy," on past the *Brown House*, crossing the old Ridgeway, till he comes to the milestone on which he had carved his name so many years before. There he spreads his blanket on the wet ground and stops to rest awhile. "He passed the spot where the gibbet of his ancestor and Sue's had stood, and descended the hill." It is late when he at length reaches *Christminster*. At the station he is met by Arabella, and we see them passing together along the street by "the silent colleges." Reminiscences crowd on him (58). "This is Old Rubric," he says. "And this Sarcophagus; and up that lane Crozier and Tudor; and all down there is Cardinal with its long front, and its windows with lifted eyebrows." If we pass down St. Aldate's Street we may stand awhile and conjecture which of the colleges before us are most appropriately served by the factitious names our author bestows on them. Certainly we shall not be very wide of the mark in supposing that *Cardinal* is more or less representative of Christ Church, when the others will naturally drop into their respective places.

The action is again at *Marygreen* for the last time; and then *Christminster* holds us for the final scene. It is the death-bed of Jude. The house in which he finally lives, and in which he dies, we cannot find; it was in the central portion of the town and at no great distance from the Sheldonian Theatre (59). Let that approximation suffice; we have already torn the veil somewhat ruthlessly in our endeavour to discover the real and to make it conterminous with the counterfeit.

CHAPTER IV

THE action of this story is limited to a very circumscribed area, so that the old dramatic quality—unity of place—is deeply marked throughout. The backgrounds are drawn essentially from Nature and few objects of architectural interest intrude. The characters which figure are, with perhaps one exception, entirely in harmony with their environment, and it would be difficult to imagine a more congruous setting for them than that of *Egdon Heath*. This book, which is deemed by some to be Mr. Hardy's masterpiece in prose, gives us convincing proof of our author's appreciation of, and sympathy with, Nature. It is Nature pure, Nature simple, yet illimitable and mysterious.

Egdon Heath represents that vast expanse of moorland which stretches, practically without a break, from Dorchester to Bournemouth. Its natural, untamable wildness is the charm that makes it so subtly attractive, for it defies all attempts at subjugation—except in a few isolated spots, and even then the efforts to cultivate it have involved an amount of labour and expense which is scarcely justified by the results. It is unconquered and unconquerable by agriculture, and more immutable in character than any other part of the Wessex country (60).

To those who appreciate it, the heath is beautiful at all hours of the day, whether in sunlight or in shade, and at all seasons of the year ; but if we would see it in the guise in which it appears in the book before us we must view it at the "transitional point of its nightly roll into darkness"; for we are told "nobody could be said to understand the heath who had not been there at such a time."

As is known to readers, the centre and apex of *Egdon Heath* in the novel is the lofty hill called Rainbarrow. In point of fact the barrow from which this is taken and named is not in the middle of the heath by a long way, but nearly on the western edge. But, apparently to give more of the general effect, it is assumed to be somewhat farther in, at some similar spot where the outlook is more exclusively heathland.

The present writer once spent a night on the barrow, arriving there just before the sun sank behind the tops of *Yalbury Firs*, and watched as "the obscurity in the air and the obscurity in the land closed together in a black fraternization towards which each advanced half-way." It was then that an on-looker could grasp the full significance of its mysterious individuality; could mark how "the place became full of a watchful intentness"; how "the heath appeared slowly to awake and listen." The moon rose from behind the water-meadows that reach out widely on both sides of the river Froom, a creamy light flooding the pool wherein Eustacia Vye was said to have been drowned, gilding the roof-ridge of the *Quiet Woman* Inn, and intensifying "the sombre stretch of rounds and hollows" of which the heath was composed. All was very still, save for the occasional low of a cow from the vale beneath, now wrapped in a winding sheet of white mist. An owl sailed by on muffled wings, silhouetted darkly against the moonlit sky; night-hawks and bats darted hither and thither. Gradually the hours passed, until there seemed to come a struggle on the part of Nature, and an eerie feeling seemed to suggest that "something was about to happen." After a time the tenseness gave place to a sense of relaxation: as though itself sentient, the

60.—WAREHAM HEATH.

61.—PUDDLETOWN HEATH.

shadowy heath appeared to be conscious that the strain was past, and the breeze which stole gently out of the flushing east seemed to the watcher like a sigh of relief coming forth from its very core. And behold it was dawn. But long before the faintest glimmer of daylight touched the sky the herons were awake in the fir-clump near by in the direction of peaceful *Blooms-End*; and they screamed harsh, guttural cries as they rose from the trees and flew down into the mist-laden meadows to fish.

Egdon seldom wears the same aspect for long; sensitive to the slightest change of atmospheric influence, it seems to reflect Nature's every vagary, to adapt itself as it were to Nature's every mood. In spring the predominant tone is purplish-brown; in summer its purple-red body-colour is patched with green in every conceivable shade; in autumn it displays an orange colour-scheme; while in winter we find russet-browns prevailing, though the heather still carries sufficient purple tinge to be reminiscent of the summer past, and in the hollows the shadows are blue-black and full of lustre.

It does not require a very vivid imagination to picture the effect which *Egdon Heath* must have had on our author when we realise that much of his early life was passed on its very margin; nor can we be surprised that he should have absorbed the atmosphere which belongs to it. The active influence of the heath is marked in many ways by its bearing on the characters. To Eustacia Vye it was a foreign land, for " Budmouth (Weymouth) was her native place, a fashionable seaside resort at that date." To Clym Yeobright it was home itself. " Take all the various hates felt by Eustacia Vye towards the heath and translate them into loves, and you have the heart of Clym."

Practically all the incidents take place on *Egdon*; in its wild centre was enacted the mingled tragedy and comedy which made up the lives of the several characters—amid its ancient barrows, its crater-like pits, its rushy pools, under its lichen-shrouded thorns, on its heights, in its valleys. The heath forms a background for many of the scenes in " The Dynasts," " Tess of the d'Urbervilles," " The Fiddler of the Reels," and several pieces of narrative verse.

We will now proceed to explore the heath and view such portions and features as served for the imaginative places described in the book. By taking the London Road out of Dorchester and bearing to the right at the top of Stinsford Hill we shall come, in the course of three miles, to a road turning somewhat abruptly to the left and leading in due course to Puddletown, passing Coomb-Firtrees (see the poem entitled "Yell'ham Wood's Story ") on the way. This road strikes us at once as being typical of the "aged highway" along which Captain Vye is supposed to have been walking when he was overtaken by Diggory Venn, the Reddleman. "Before him stretched the long, laborious road, dry, empty, and white. It was quite open to the heath on each side, and bisected that vast dark surface like the parting-line on a head of black hair, diminishing and bending away on the furthest horizon " (61).

It is rare nowadays to meet any one travelling about the country with reddle to sell, but some twenty years ago an occasional vendor might have been seen. Probably the last member of that class is an old woman named Mary-Ann Bull, who, with her ancient pony and still more ancient vehicle, wends her solitary way through Dorset and the adjoining counties, selling silver-sand, 'peat, reddle, and such-like commodities. Reddle, which is a red chalk, was once extensively used by shepherds for marking their sheep, and at one time farmers were practically dependent on the travelling vendor for their supplies.

The " heath-croppers," those hardy, shaggy animals which drew the Reddleman's van, were once quite common on *Egdon Heath*, but are never seen now, mainly perhaps because many of the ancient common rights have become vested in the lords of the manors.

According to the narrative, the Reddleman had travelled a long distance that day—from *Anglebury*,—which is approximately Wareham—following a road which would have kept him in sight of the heath the whole way. The old road from Wareham to Puddletown crosses the very centre of the *Egdon* expanse, running mostly on the ridge of the hills, with the Froom valley on the left hand and the Pydel valley on the right hand, the latter backed by *Greenhill*—familiar to us in " Far from the Madding Crowd "—Weatherbury Castle, and other landmarks which claim our attention from time to time.

If we will follow Captain Vye and the Reddleman as they pursue their way, we shall see on our left hand the tumuli called Rainbarrows, of which we may consider the largest as representative of the Rainbarrow of the story, although we are inclined to surmise from certain suggestive descriptions that, as we have already hinted, in our author's imagination it stood in a more central portion of *Egdon Heath* ; for he says of it : " This bossy projection of earth above its natural level occupied the loftiest ground of the loneliest height that the heath contained. . . . It formed the pole and axis of this heathery world. . . . Above the plain rose the hill, above the hill rose the barrow " (62).

Although the word barrow denotes a mound or hillock in its most literal sense, the term is now employed almost exclusively to signify a burial-place. It was on the top of Rainbarrow that the bonfire was kindled. This method of celebrating historic episodes of the past, which doubtless had its origin in prehistoric times and was directly connected with ceremonies of a religious nature, is now seldom seen. We shall examine the barrow more critically when we come to our chapter on the country of " The Dynasts," where it is again the scene of a fire. The only other illumination which concerns us just now is the little fire supposed to have

62.—RAINBARROW.

63.—THE DUCK DAIRY HOUSE.

73

been lighted by Eustacia Vye on a mound in front of her grandfather's house at *Mistover Knap*—a spot that can be guessed at with some exactitude as being "at the junction of two converging bank fences" to the north of Rainbarrow.

To the group here assembled comes the Reddleman, inquiring his way to *Blooms-End*, and causing consternation by reason of his red attire and his realistic likeness to the "red ghost" seen by the little boy and described by Timothy Fairway. The apparition alarmed Susan Nonsuch also, for she "had a dream last night of a death's-head." This superstitious dread calls to mind an authentic case of an old woman who, when she was a child, used to walk three miles night and morning across the heath to attend school. The only thing she was ever "a-veared o'" was lest "a death's-head" should alight on her and suck her blood! It is obvious that this harmless moth was in her estimation as dangerous as *desmodus rufus*, the blood-sucking bat.

Following the ghosts of the bygone company as they descend to the *Quiet Woman Inn* to "strike up a ballet in front of the married folks' door," we shall find no longer an inn but a dairy-house, known to-day as "The Duck." Once upon a time it was "The Wild Duck Inn," and, earlier still, "Travellers' Rest," and had a secret hiding-place for smuggled goods. Two loose floor-boards in the upper story gave access to a cavity in the walls, undiscernible from below. The intermediate wall was afterwards removed, but on the ceiling we can still trace the spot where the opening once was. Evidence of the house having been an inn originally is shown by a little hatch in the wall separating the parlour from the kitchen. Through it many foaming pots of ale used to pass at the time when the story was written (63). The *Quiet Woman* figures many times in the course of the narrative, as also in the short tale entitled "The Fiddler of the Reels." It should be added that some features of its description in the novel are borrowed from a largely similar inn—"The Red Lion," of Winfrith—also once the haunt of smugglers, and a suggestive spot still.

Mistover Knap was supposed to be only a short distance from Rainbarrow. Nothing definite remains to mark where the house originally stood, but we read that close to it "there was a large pool, bearded all round by heather and rushes." Such a pool, answering to the description given, may be found to the north of the barrows, close under a bank. The remains of an old closed brick-kiln are in a hollow near. Here our author imagines Eustacia Vye to have resided—the character described as the "raw material of a divinity," possessed of "Pagan eyes, full of nocturnal mysteries." *Mistover* was the fictitious name given to a few houses which were scattered upon the heath in this locality; but being built only of mud (*i.e.* clay mixed with chalk and held together with heather-stems, tough grasses, straw, etc.), they have completely disappeared. As long as the roof is kept in good repair these mud-walled houses will last for a long time, but directly that becomes defective the walls literally melt away. This method of building is now practically a lost art; very few, even of the older labourers, possess the requisite knowledge and skill. The fir trees which backed the dwelling on *Mistover Knap* have likewise disappeared —burned in one of the fires which ravage the heath at intervals.

Blooms-End, the name given to the home of the Yeobrights, was drawn from a farm-house called Bhompston, which stands in a grass field just off the margin of the heath in the direction of Lower Bock-hampton village. Its front is much altered now from that of the "irregular, thatched house" of the story, and the white palings that once enclosed it have disappeared, but there still remain certain characteristics, particularly at the back, which will serve to remind us of the time when the mummers were supposed to have stood in the old oak-beamed room and played "St.

George and the Dragon" at the Christmas revels (64).
Mumming, or momming, was common in mediæval
England, and was probably a survival of the Roman
masquerade which took place during the orgies of
Saturnalia. A spurious imitation, little more than a
parody on the original, was occasionally met with a
few years back, but the performance was never given
with the seriousness usual to it a century or less ago.

There are many curious conical pits on *Egdon
Heath*, some being of great depth, and with abrupt,
regular sides. A typical one is that known as "Cul-
pepper's Dish," near Briantspuddle, and at no great
distance from the cottage which we shall examine
later under the name of *Alderworth*. One of these
pits forms the background for a short scene when
Mrs. Yeobright and Thomasin go to gather holly for
the decorations. It was at "the place where the
hollies grew, which was in a conical pit, so that the
tops of the trees were not much above the general
level of the ground." This is a very accurate description of many such pits, and was probably taken from
no one in particular.

The church at which Wildeve and Thomasin were
supposed to be married may perhaps be regarded as
Mellstock (Stinsford)— to be referred to more fully in
subsequent chapters. It will be remembered that the
arrangement to marry at *Anglebury* had fallen through,
but on the day newly appointed we see Thomasin
setting out to walk to the church, and appearing as
"a little figure wending its way between the scratching
furze bushes . . ., a pale-blue spot in a vast field of
natural brown."

Many of the old-time Wessex customs mentioned
in the novels have now become extinct, or nearly so,
but one which still flourishes with unabated vigour is
the "hair-cutting," referred to in the present story.
The Fairways of to-day have altered very little, their
methods are still primitive, and almost any Sunday
morning we may light upon a similar scene to that

64.—Bhompston Farm.

65.—Affpuddle Church.

77

described in the book before us. We may then see "the victim sitting on a chopping-block . . . and the neighbours gossiping around." It was at this function that Clym joined the group, and mentioned his determination to "keep a school as near to Egdon as possible."

Another episode which interests us is that of Susan pricking Eustacia with a stocking-needle while in church, on the supposition that she was a witch. This belief in witchcraft will be noticed more fully in a future chapter, where we deal with the story entitled " The Withered Arm." The custom of " blood-drawing " was supposed to constitute the most effective remedy when a person was "overlooked" by another; and if only the witch's blood could be drawn nothing further need be feared. This practice is resorted to occasionally even now in Wessex, and some authentic instances have come before the present writer within the past few years.

Alderworth is the fictitious name of the cottage which Clym is supposed to have rented after his marriage to Eustacia. It was situated " near a village about five miles off " in the direction of *East Egdon* village. It was at the church in this village that they were married, and we venture to claim it as Affpuddle (65). *Alderworth* is in a lonely situation; we are told "it was almost as lonely as that of Eustacia's grandfather, but the fact that it stood near a heath was disguised by a belt of firs which almost enclosed the premises." In order to reach it, Clym would have traced backwards for some distance the road by which the Reddleman had reached *Rainbarrow* from *Anglebury*. Through *Stickleford*, under Clyffe Clump—a feature occurring in the poem titled " Yell'ham Wood's Story " —and thence along the old Wareham Road until Moreton North Lodge was reached; from there a turning to the left hand, and a subsequent bearing to the left again, would lead directly to the cottage (66).

We now read of the " village festivity " to which

66.—Brickyard Cottage, Affpuddle Heath.

67.—Throop Corner.

Eustacia went one afternoon and met Wildeve. He afterwards escorted her homewards as far as Throop Corner, near which place they saw Clym and Diggory Venn (67). We are unable to locate the actual spot where the dancing took place, but we can readily find Throop Corner—the junction of four cross-roads, of which the northern one leads down the steep declivity into the hamlet of Throop.

Let us follow Mrs. Yeobright as she goes on a broiling day in August to visit Clym at *Alderworth.* "The sun had branded the whole heath with his mark." Tired, weak, often mistaking the way and frequently taking wrong paths, she is presently directed to pursue an individual ahead of her, and whom she at length recognises as her son. She watches him enter the cottage, and then stays to rest awhile under a clump of trees on a knoll; "the place was called the Devil's Bellows." Probably such a knoll existed at the time of the narrative, but we cannot now mark its site with exactness. It was on her return journey that, weak and tired-out, she collapsed and lay on the ground near the path. Here Clym finds her later in the day as he is walking towards *Blooms-End,* and we see him carrying her unconscious form and laying it down in the hut "built of clods and covered with thin turves." She had been bitten on her ankle by an adder, and the remedy suggested by Sam was duly tried. "You must rub the place with the fat of other adders, and the only way to get that is by frying them," he said. But in spite of all their efforts she dies shortly.

This remedy, as our author points out, is a very ancient one. It is still spoken of in Wessex, and occasionally resorted to. Naturally, science of the present day would scoff at such an "old woman's" specific, but nevertheless there are instances on record where it has been known to effect, or aid in, a cure. The separation of mental and physical phenomena cannot be arbitrarily defined, and it is surely not impossible that there may be a material effect in a remedy in which faith plays a prominent part.

A fresh background is before us in the scene of another tragedy. " Shadwater Weir had at its foot a large circular pool, fifty feet in diameter, into which the water flowed through ten large hatches." The actual weir which provided our author with his model may be found in the meadows behind Woodsford Castle, and it can be reached either from that place

68.—THE WEIR, WOODSFORD MEADOWS.

or by a lane leading from the *Quiet Woman* (68). It takes the whole water of the river Froom. In summer weather, when the rainfall is low, the water merely glides through the hatches in a calm even stream, the sun shining through the clear water and illuminating the gravelled bottom ; but in winter the pool is a boiling cauldron, the flood of water rushes with terrific force, the pool is coated with foam. There has been very little change here since the time when, according to the story, Eustacia Vye was drowned and Wildeve lost his own life in an attempt to rescue her; but probably our author imagined it considerably nearer to the *Quiet Woman* than it actually is.

We read of Diggory Venn's marriage to Thomasin, and their subsequent residence in the dairy at *Stickle-ford*, a place which may be likened to Tincleton. A visit here will show us a picturesque farm-house of stone, with heavy chimneys, and a general appearance of solidity, which we may surmise served for the dairy-house.

The background for the final scene is again Rain-barrow. Clym is before us—"a motionless figure standing on the top of the tumulus, just as Eustacia had stood on that lonely summit some two years and a half before." And in fancy we can see him there, surrounded by many of his neighbours, who lie at their ease on the heather and listen to the words that fall from his lips. Here he has fixed his pulpit, and his roofless church is typified by the wild expanse of *Egdon Heath*.

CHAPTER V

As we might expect from the title, the interest of this story centres in *Casterbridge*, a name which we have grown to look on as being synonymous with Dorchester; and it is here, in the capital town of South Wessex, that most of the action takes place. The book before us was first published in volume form in 1886, and it should be noted in passing that the late editions contain nearly a whole chapter more than the first. The story is essentially a biography, the main interest lying around the personality of Michael Henchard, the Mayor.

The surroundings are so graphically and faithfully described that the concrete forms of natural and artificial features which serve as models for the fictitious creations take to themselves the appearance of realities. Some of these, for the more convenient staging of the story, have been tampered with to the extent of moving them a short distance from their actual positions; but this applies only to certain houses, the natural landmarks remain consistently *in situ*. That some of the more ancient houses and other configurations have been altered, demolished, or displaced by more modern structures, is a regrettable fact which the archæologist must face; though such substitutions would seem to be inseparable from the usual progress of civilisation. Future generations will doubtless realise that these metamorphoses of old towns should be denoted by a term as strong as, or stronger than, vandalism, since the larger proportion are not the outcome of necessity, but the result of a mere destructive policy.

The story opens at *Weydon Priors*—presumably Weyhill—in Upper Wessex, where is enacted the episode of the wife-selling, an incident, it may be mentioned, which is by no means without parallel. The fair is held close to the village of Weyhill. "The spot stretched downward into valleys and onward to other uplands, dotted with barrows and trenched with the remains of prehistoric forts"—a description easily verified to-day. Although a fair is still held there thrice annually, it has steadily declined in magnitude and interest, like all similar institutions; but, nevertheless, Weyhill still holds its record as being the most important sheep-fair in the county, and the visitor to-day may still meet with the "peep-shows, toy-stands, wax-works, inspired monsters, disinterested medical men who travelled for the public good, thimble-riggers, nick-nack vendors and readers of Fate"—if not in entirety at least in part. For the "good home-brewed beer, ale, and cider" we shall find it useless to ask. The "good furmity" is likewise no longer obtainable (69).

It is generally supposed that a fair in its inception had a distinct connection with ecclesiasticism, many of the fair-days being synchronous with feast-days of the Church, but there exists fairly conclusive evidence to prove that they were instituted anteriorly to the establishment of Church dogma. Although we know fairs were in existence long before the date of the Norman Conquest, it was only subsequently that they became of capital importance or were held under charter. The first grant mentioned was in the reign of William I., who accorded to the Bishop of Winchester the prescriptive right to hold an annual "free fair" at St. Giles' Hill.

The principal fair at Weyhill is held on the 10th of

69.—The Fair Ground, Weyhill.

70.—Dorchester from the East.

October, and to it come buyers and sellers from long distances. The booths here are permanent structures, built of brick or cob-walls with either slate or iron roofs. Some of the buildings were erected many years ago, and they are still kept in a reasonable state of repair. There are two long double rows of these huts, forming, as it were, two parallel streets; their capacity being augmented by canvas and other removable erections.

As is to be expected, many old customs prevailed in connection with the old-time fairs. At the inn at Weyhill may be seen a pair of sheep-horns of perhaps the third year's growth, well curled, and having a brass cup fixed on to the forehead between them. I believe they are never used now, but at the time when hops formed an important trade here a draught from the cup was one of the integral rites which admitted a new member to the society to which it belonged. There was a recognised song, too long to quote in full, but of which we may give the chorus:

> So fleet runs the hare, and so cunning runs the fox;
> Why shouldn't this young calf live to grow an ox,
> Oh, for to get his living among briars and thorns,
> And drink like his daddy with his large pair of horns.
>> Horns, boys, horns;
>> Horns, boys, horns,
> And die like his daddy with his large pair of horns.

On the morning following the sale of his wife, Henchard is said to have started in search of her and the little child, now under the guardianship of Newson; but ere he commences his quest we see him entering a church, and there taking a solemn oath to "avoid all strong liquors for the space of twenty years to come." The church in which he registered his oath receives no exact description, and its position can therefore not be pointed out. For many months he pursues his fruitless search, until at last, disappointed, almost despairing of success, he strikes out in a straight line for *Casterbridge*. We may well suppose that the seaport at which he ended his search was South-ampton, since we read that "Next day he started, journeying south-westward, and did not pause, except for nights' lodgings, till he reached the town of Caster-bridge, in a far distant part of Wessex."

Some sixteen or seventeen years subsequent to this date we are again at the fair of *Weydon Priors*, in company with Henchard's wife and Elizabeth-Jane, but only for quite a short time; they had come to elicit information regarding Henchard's whereabouts, and from the old Furmity Woman they learned that he had left a message with her, in case of inquiries being made, to the effect that "he'd gone to—where?—Casterbridge."

We follow Mrs. Henchard and Elizabeth-Jane as they proceed thither. By walking, and occasionally obtaining a lift in a waggon or carrier's van, they in due course draw near to *Casterbridge*.

It was just before dusk on an evening in mid-September that they paused to rest on the summit of a hill. "The spot commanded a full view of the town and its environs." The vantage point they had reached was assuredly Stinsford Hill—familiar to Hardy readers as *Mellstock Rise*, this name associating it with *Mellstock Village* close by, and the adjacent country inhabited by the members of the *Mellstock Quire*, to whom we are introduced in the book entitled "Under the Greenwood Tree."

To Elizabeth-Jane the town appeared as "an old-fashioned place . . . huddled all together . . . shut in by a square mass of trees, like a plot of garden ground by a box edging." Our author further says of it: "To birds of a more soaring kind, Casterbridge must have appeared on this fine evening as a mosaic work of subdued reds, browns, greys, and crystals, held together by a rectangular frame of deep green," and if we climb to the summit of Stinsford Hill on any clear evening in autumn, we shall be struck with the simili-tude of the view that stretches before us and the one described. So life-like is the presentment, we can almost persuade ourselves the clock has stood still, that we are living contemporaneously with Henchard, and Farfrae, and Elizabeth-Jane.

Having rested there awhile they went on. "The dense trees of the avenue rendered the road dark as a tunnel . . . they passed down a midnight between two gloamings." It must be noted with regret that the fine old elms which formed the avenue on the London Road were broken and uprooted during some of the north-westerly gales about twenty years ago (70). Younger trees have taken the place of the old, but it will be many years before these will give even an approximate idea of the tunnel-like appearance which it possessed formerly, and which may still be seen exemplified on the Bridport Road as it leaves Dorchester on the western side of the town.

After wandering about the town, here and there, Elizabeth-Jane and her mother sought the High Street. There were "timber houses with over-hanging stories . . . there were houses of brick-nogging . . . there were slate roofs patched with tiles, and tile roofs patched with slate, and occasionally a roof of thatch." Instances of these last may still be seen, though most of this wayward, irresponsible architecture has been swept away since the days of Henchard's supposed mayoralty.

Before we follow our characters farther, or identify the places mentioned in connection with them, it may be interesting to glance briefly at the historical associations of the town. The most ancient name by which it was known was *Durnovaria*, clearly of Celtic origin. Its occupation by the Romans would seem to have been a long one, for the whole district teems with relics of Roman buildings, walls, villas, roads, coins, and pottery; but it is generally held that prior to the Roman entry it was a tribal centre of the *Durotriges*, Maiden Castle being regarded as their great stronghold. We have little precise history of

Dorchester in Saxon times, when it was called
Dornceaster or *Dorcestre*, but there is mention of a
charter to Milton Abbey, given by Æthelstan in 939,
as having come from Doracestria, which at that time
purported to be a royal town, and was possessed of a
mint. Its present name is of course traceable to the
Roman influence. In the year 1613 the town was
almost completely destroyed by fire. With some of
its later historical connections we shall be concerned
presently.

Returning to our wayfarers, we see them standing
before "a grizzled church, whose massive square tower
rose unbroken into the darkening sky." In this we
recognise the Perpendicular Church of St. Peter, from
whose belfry the curfew bell still rings, though this
is no longer regarded as the signal for shutting the
shops! It is said by some archæologists that St.
Peter's Church is built on the site of a Roman
Temple. There is some trans-Norman work in the
arch spanning the door of the south porch. Inside
are some interesting effigies; the Hardy Chapel at
the end of the south aisle brings back to us forcibly
our author's connection with the town through his
ancestors. In the close will be seen the bronze statue
erected to the memory of William Barnes.

"Other clocks struck eight from time to time;
one gloomily from the gaol, another from the gable
of an almshouse. . . ." The gaol, which interests us
more particularly in the story entitled "The Withered
Arm," stands on the site once occupied by a Norman
Castle, of which we find mention in records of the
twelfth and thirteenth centuries. The short, steep
hill which ascends from the river is called Castle Hill
to-day. The Almshouse is doubtless the one in
South Street, known as Napier's or Napper's Mite.

Our next halt is in front of the King's Arms Hotel
(figuring under its rightful name). Its "spacious bow-
window projected into the street over the main portico,"
and does so still (71). Here Farfrae comes on the scene,

and in reply to his inquiry for "a respectable hotel
. . . more moderate than this," he is recommended
to "The Three Mariners, just below." This hostel,
with its "two prominent gables, bow-window, and
passage light," has been pulled down since the book
was written, but certain features may still be traced
in the "four-centred Tudor arch" which leads into
the stable-yard.

Passing up the High Street the day following,
Elizabeth-Jane took notice of the carriers' vans which
hailed "from Mellstock (Bockhampton), Weatherbury
(Puddletown), The Hintocks (Minterne, etc.), Sherton
Abbas (Sherborne), Kingsbere (Bere Regis), Overcombe (partly Upwey), and many other towns and
villages round." These vans form a particularly
noticeable feature in Dorchester, and may also be
seen in Salisbury and many other ancient market
towns in Wessex. But the penned pigs and the rows
of horses no longer fill the High Street on fair-days,
and must be sought for in the market-field.

The house in which Henchard lived was, we read,
"one of the best, faced with dull red and grey old
brick." Such a house may be seen in South Street,
standing a little back from the pavement, its rear pointing towards *Durnover* (supposititiously Fordington),
where stood the barns and granaries which pertained
to the corn merchant's trade. Just previous to
Elizabeth's visit there to find Henchard, we see him,
in company with Farfrae, passing up the High Street
to Top o' Town, bearing suddenly to the right, and
turning "down an avenue on the town wall called
Chalk Walk (probably Colliton Walk), leading to an
angle where the north and west escarpments met" (72).
These walks are in reality boulevards, being placed
exactly on the top of the actual earthen vallum
thrown up by the Romans when they fortified the
town. As late as the end of the eighteenth century
considerable lengths of the Roman stone wall were
found. On the east the great walls were actually

71.—THE KING'S ARMS, DORCHESTER.

72.—THE BATH AND BRISTOL ROAD, DORCHESTER.

grubbed up, partly because they formed an obstruction, and partly in order that the avenues of trees might be planted thereon.

Our next background is the place where Henchard agreed to meet his wife. " The Ring at Casterbridge was merely the local name of one of the finest Roman Amphitheatres, if not the very finest, remaining in Britain " (73). In the Wessex poem entitled " Her Death and After " it is referred to as the *Cirque of the Gladiators.* At this point in the narrative we are reminded of the tremendous influence the Roman occupation had on Dorchester. " Casterbridge announced old Rome in every street, alley, and precinct. It looked Roman, bespoke the art of Rome, concealed dead men of Rome." The building of Mr. Hardy's house at Max Gate brought to light many Roman relics, including several ancient graves in which were coins, pottery, urns, etc. Maumbury Rings is an alternative title by which the Amphitheatre is known—a name connected perhaps with the word mummery. Recent excavations have brought to light many interesting points in connection with its origin and its purpose : an account of these researches may be obtained from the County Museum at Dorchester. It was here, at this spot so charged with ancient reminiscences, that the husband and wife were said to meet after dusk had fallen, and at the end of their interview Henchard recommended Susan to take lodgings for the time being "over the china shop in High Street." We may find this house almost opposite the County Museum, joining to the house known as Judge Jeffreys' Lodgings—the place where he lodged during the Bloody Assizes. The lower part is still used as a china shop. The Amphitheatre also serves as a meeting-place for Henchard and Lucetta later on in the narrative.

At the date of the story, Dorchester was enclosed in a much more restricted area, the streets were narrower, the houses were more tightly packed. It

73.—THE AMPHITHEATRE, DORCHESTER.

74.—THE WEST WALKS, DORCHESTER.

was "a place deposited in a block upon a corn-field."
At that time Fordington appears to have been the
centre of the agricultural interests, for we read that
" wheat ricks overhung the old Roman street and thrust
their eaves against the church tower ; green thatched
barns, with doorways as high as the gates of Solomon's
temple, opened directly upon the main thoroughfare."
It was in one of these granaries on *Durnover Hill*
(Fordington Hill), situated at the back of Henchard's
house, and close to the church, that Elizabeth-Jane's
meeting with Farfrae is described. The "humpbacked
barn, cushioned with moss, and the granary, rising
against the church tower behind," have disappeared
completely. They were demolished in order to make
room for the new rectory, and also because they stood
so close to the church as to throw an awkward shade
and darken the windows.

The Antelope Hotel (known by its real name) is an
interesting old hostel of the seventeenth century, to be
found on the side of South Street opposite to where
Henchard's house stands, but a little nearer Cornhill.
It interests us only as being the place appointed by
Lucetta for her first interview with Henchard.

If we continue to follow the events in the order
related, we shall now find ourselves confronted with
the rival entertainments of Henchard and Farfrae.
" Close to the town was an elevated green spot surrounded by an ancient square earthwork." This was
Pummery or Poundbury, and represented the site
chosen by Henchard as being a suitable spot for his
merry-making. There is much controversy regarding
the origin of this earthwork, antiquarian experts placing
it as British, Roman, Danish—according to individual
conviction ; while others hold that it probably partakes
of all three epochs and was severally occupied and
altered at three distinct periods. It lies just outside
the town to the north-west. Farfrae's opposition fête
was held in the West Walks—still so called (74). At its
termination we see Farfrae escorting Elizabeth-Jane

75.—The River Path, Dorchester.

76.—Friary Mill, Dorchester.

95

home, passing "down the West Walk, and then into the Bowling Walk," and thus up South Street. Bowling Walk is another of the features that shows under the same title to-day.

The *Corn Market*—a place which figures conspicuously in "Far from the Madding Crowd"—is also frequently mentioned here. At the time when Henchard was ostensibly mayor, this particular section of the town wore a very different aspect. The roadway passing between the present corn exchange and St. Peter's Church was at that time spanned by an arch connecting the two buildings. *Bull-stake Square* (North Square), to which the arch gave entrance, had a stone post in its centre, and to it the bull was tied for baiting. Bull-baiting, it may be noted, was only put a stop to by Act of Parliament in 1835. Here, too, were the stocks—now reposing in the County Museum —and likewise the old town pump which now stands in Cornhill. In the story this formed a favourite meeting-place for Mother Cuxsom, Solomon Longways, and the other gossips of the town.

After the death of Mrs. Henchard, and the reading of the letter of confession which she left behind her, we see her husband in a morbid frame of mind leaving the house and passing down the street until he reaches a bridge. Thence he follows the path beside the river (75). "These precincts embodied the mournful phases of Casterbridge life. . . . Here were ruins of a Franciscan Priory." In the darkness, passing the old County gaol —not to be confounded with the present building— with the sound of the roaring weir in his ears and his mind full of unrest, he reaches the cottage where the local hangman lived, climbs up the steep hill called Glydepath Rise, and re-enters the town.

All this part of Dorchester is naturally much altered since the date assumed for the story, but we may still see sufficient realism to bring the scene back to our minds. The old brick bridge, from which the pathway leads, will be referred to later on. Friary Mill, once

77.—Weir Hole near Friary Mill, Dorchester.

78.—Colliton House, Dorchester.

attached to the Franciscan Priory, still exhibits a certain picturesqueness, though modern disregard for the beautiful in favour of the merely utilitarian has denuded it of many old salient features (76). It is supposed to stand close to the site of a Norman castle and to be built partly out of the stones that once formed the castle walls.

A little way beyond the mill is a deep hole, darkly shadowed by willow trees; this we may regard as the place "wherein nameless infants had been used to disappear" (77). Still following the river path and passing the present gaol, we soon see before us a picturesque thatched cottage, still known as the hangman's cottage. But as this bulks more largely in the short story entitled "The Withered Arm" we shall examine it more closely in a later chapter. Close beside it is a weir over which the water pours with considerable force, emitting the roar which assailed Henchard's ears.

On *Durnover Hill* (Fordington Hill) we come upon the cemetery in which it is alleged Susan Henchard was interred—"a churchyard old as civilisation. . . . Mrs. Henchard's dust mingled with the dust of women who lay ornamented with glass hairpins and amber necklaces, and men who held in their mouths coins of Hadrian, Posthumus, and the Constantines," says our author, thus reminding us again of the Roman connection with Dorchester. Some late alterations to Fordington Church have disclosed a stone slab bearing the names of certain Roman citizens carved in Roman type. It was here that Elizabeth-Jane supposedly came to visit her mother's grave, and made her first acquaintance with Lucetta.

High Place Hall, the residence of Lucetta, was apparently drawn from Colliton House (78). Its actual position, however, must be imagined farther eastwards, towards North Square. "The Hall, with its grey *façade* and parapet . . . was entirely of stone . . . its rooms overlooked the market-place. . . ." One of its most curious and interesting features is the bricked-up

79.—The Mask, Colliton House.

80.—Damer's Barn, Dorchester.

99

doorway in the wall and the mask which adorns the key-stone (79). "Originally the mask had exhibited a comic leer, as could still be discovered; but generations of Casterbridge boys had thrown stones at the mask, aiming at its open mouth, and the blows thereof had chipped off the lips and jaws as if they had been eaten away by a disease." In this house Elizabeth-Jane is said to take up her residence, and many interesting scenes are staged within its walls and in the market-place which its windows overlooked. The Museum, to which she was sent by Lucetta soon after her arrival, was "an old house in a back street. There are crowds of interesting things—skeletons, teeth, old pots and pans, ancient boots and shoes, birds' eggs—all charm-ingly instructive." The place mentioned must not be confounded with the present County Museum, but must be sought for in a house in Trinity Street, adjacent to the stable-yard of the Antelope Hotel.

Lucetta's visit to *Port-Bredy* (Bridport) leads directly to the scene in the barn on the Bridport Road. It is known as Damer's Barn, and it lies in the dip of the hill just at the end of the west avenue (80). "The spot was a vale between two gentle acclivities, and the road, still adhering to its Roman foundation, stretched onward straight as a surveyor's line till lost to sight on the most distant ridge,"—a statement verified by a visit to-day.

Our interest is now claimed by those portions of *Casterbridge* which were said to be frequented by the less prosperous inhabitants. "Two bridges stood near the lower part of Casterbridge town. The first, of weather-stained brick, was immediately at the end of High Street (the eastern extremity) (81). . . . The second bridge, of stone, was farther out on the high-way" (82). The description given in the book is as true to-day as when it was written. An examination of the actual fabric discloses the evidence of that peculiar wear and tear due to the unconscious leanings and rubbings and heel-friction; while the persons who are

81.—The Swan Bridge, Dorchester.

82.—Grey's Bridge, Dorchester.

to be seen lounging against the parapets seem still to
resemble the types referred to in a marked degree.
With the habitués of the brick-built bridge—that one
just at the bottom of the town—must be included
those "of the lowest character." On the stone bridge
—Grey's Bridge, farther down the London Road—we
find a different set of loiterers : "the miserables who
would pause on the remoter bridge were of a politer
stamp. They included bankrupts, hypochondriacs . . .
shabby-genteel men." These bridges are important
features and receive mention in several of the novels
and poems.

To those who love realism for its own sake, *Mixen
Lane* (Mill Street) will come as a disappointment.
Even at the time when the story was written this
section of *Casterbridge* was in a stage of transition,
and to-day there only remain slight indications of its
original sordid character. Many of the houses have
been pulled down, condemned as unfit for human
habitation ; the moral atmosphere has to a large extent
been similarly purged, and a special mission has lately
been inaugurated, having for its object the cleansing
of this Augean Stable (83). "Mixen Lane was the
Adullam of all the surrounding villages. . . . The
Inn called Peter's Finger was the church of Mixen
Lane." This inn has been demolished, like so many
of the houses in Mill Street. Its name may be found
in the inn at Lytchett Minster a building figuring in
"The Hand of Ethelberta"—where the hanging sign
is supposedly a portrait of *St. Peter ad Vincula*. It is
here, in *Mixen Lane*, we are introduced to some of
the shadier characters which form the appendages to
Henchard. Jopp, the Furmity Woman, Mother
Cuxsom, Nance Mockridge—all had their residences
around the inn, and it was inside this little hostel that
"the skimmity ride" was planned. This curious
custom is now extinct, but the present writer can
remember such a function taking place in more than
one village near Dorchester within the last twenty-

83.—THE BACK OF MILL STREET, DORCHESTER.

84.—TEN HATCHES WEIR, DORCHESTER.

five years, and many people are still alive who have actually taken a part in the processions. The result of the "skimmity ride" was even greater than the originators had planned, Lucetta—now Mrs. Farfrae—being stricken down by the shock and expiring shortly after the procession had passed beneath her window. It was after learning of her seizure that Henchard set off to try to find Farfrae and expedite his return. We see him hastening through the town, crossing *Durnover Moor*, and climbing *Mellstock Hill*, until he reaches *Yalbury Bottom*—the base of Yellowham Hill —and instead of going straight home, proceeding up Cuckoo Lane to *Mellstock Village* (Lower Bockhampton).

Later on, as will be remembered by readers, Henchard contemplates suicide, and proceeds to *Ten Hatches Hole* for that purpose. We can see the Ten Hatches from Grey's Bridge, on the northern side of the road, and we can reach the spot by following the path which runs alongside the river. Here he discovers his effigy "in the circular pool formed by the wash of centuries—the pool he was intending to make his death-bed," and his purpose is frustrated thereby, for he superstitiously takes the effigy to be his real self. *Ten Hatches Hole* is also a feature in the poem entitled " The Curate's Kindness " (84).

We should like to identify the Corn Store near *Durnover* Church, where Henchard is supposed to have lived for a while with Elizabeth-Jane, but it has been entirely swept away. It was about this time that we read : " Elizabeth . . . often took her walks on the Budmouth (Weymouth) Road. . . . A quarter of a mile from the highway was the prehistoric fort called Mai Dun, of huge dimensions and many ramparts. . . ." We are told that Henchard often went there to watch for her appearance on the highway. This huge earthwork, which is the finest in the country, forms a feature in one of the poems and will be referred to in a later section of this book. The remaining, and perhaps the saddest, part of Henchard's career it is only necessary to recapitulate briefly. After learning of Elizabeth-Jane's determination to marry Farfrae he decides to leave *Casterbridge* and sets out at dusk, with his tool-basket slung over his shoulder and clad in his old working clothes. Elizabeth-Jane accompanies him as far as "the second bridge on the highway"—Grey's Bridge. In due course he reaches *Weydon Priors*. Here, on "the renowned hill," he mentally reconstructs the scene of his first visit, but soon the attraction of *Casterbridge*, due to his affection for Elizabeth-Jane, draws him in that direction, and we read of him circling the town, though still at some distance from it. For a time he pursues his old work of hay-trussing, labouring on a farm "near the old Western Highway," until, chancing to learn the date of the forthcoming wedding, he strikes out in a bee-line for *Casterbridge*. The second night of his journey he stops at *Shottsford*—suggestive of Blandford—where he purchases a goldfinch to take to Elizabeth-Jane as a wedding gift. At noon the next day he reaches the top of *Yalbury Hill* (Yellowham Hill), where comes to his ears "the soft pealing of the Casterbridge bells . . . a signal that all had gone well."

Next we see him at his old home, watching the dancing. His disappointment with life seemed now to reach its culminating point, and the tragedy of it pours in on his consciousness with overwhelming force, so that he turns his back on *Casterbridge* for ever.

In his track, along the *Melchester* (Salisbury) highway eastward, press Farfrae and Elizabeth-Jane, diverging from the Salisbury Road at "Weatherbury (Puddletown) by a forking highway which skirted the north of Egdon Heath." *Egdon Heath* concerns us in "The Return of the Native," and elsewhere, and it will suffice here to remark that this stretch of country extends practically from Dorchester to Bournemouth. "They searched Egdon, but found no Henchard."

They continue to search for him until they reach an "extension of the heath to the north of Anglebury (Wareham)." Here, in a cottage "built of kneaded clay," they find Henchard's body. The cottage has doubtless long passed away; the actual clump of fir trees has not disappeared; from the description we may gather that it stands on one of the highest points of Corfe Mullin heath, some twenty miles distant from Henchard's old home at *Casterbridge*.

CHAPTER VI

"THE WOODLANDERS"

THE country of "The Woodlanders" is the most per-
plexing of all the topographies in the Wessex Novels.
The action takes us to the northern portion of the
county of Dorset—or South Wessex as it is termed
in these books—on the outskirts of Blackmoor Vale.
This district is essentially one of woodlands, interspersed with wide open commons, boggy marshes,
and high grassy uplands.   It is a region inhabited by
simple-minded people, where many old-fashioned ideas
and superstitions still linger.   With the exception
of the two main roads—Dorchester-Sherborne, and
Dorchester-Yeovil—all the thoroughfares connecting
the villages are little better than lanes, most of them
winding, and some passing up and down steep hills.
Owing to the heavy nature of the soil, such lanes
become muddy and slippery in winter-time; the air
is oppressive, and produces on the traveller a curious
feeling of lassitude.   These factors combine to explain the small amount of traffic and the comparative
rarity of intrusion by strangers; they may account
also to a large extent for the meagre population, and
the prevalence and persistence of unsophisticated
thought.   Unfortunately, a retrogressive movement
is apparent to those who were familiar with the
locality thirty or more years ago; many houses and
homesteads have fallen into decay and have disappeared; the timber trade, of which we hear so

much in the story, has declined, and with it has gone
many of the smaller industries which were intimately
connected with the larger business—hollow-turning,
hurdle-making, the splitting of thatching-spars, and
the like.

In some of the Wessex Novels and Poems we can
point confidently to this or that as being the actual
model from which our author painted his word-
picture, but in the present instance it is exceedingly
difficult to identify, even approximately, many of the
features described. We are told in the preface that
the natural configurations are given under their real
names; with this to guide us we can gain a fair insight
into the position of the actual woodlands; but, in regard
to the villages and hamlets, we must content ourselves
with conjecture.

The *Hintocks* may be said to embrace Hermitage,
Hillfield, Middlemarsh, Minterne, and Melbury Bubb,
either wholly or in part, as well as certain isolated
homesteads and houses (85). The descriptions in the
book would seem to be chosen from one or other of
these places without much attempt at exact localisa-
tion; and if we choose to regard Minterne as typical
of *Great Hintock*, and Hermitage as exemplified in
Little Hintock, it must be with a certain amount of
diffidence and an acknowledgment that these designa-
tions are by no means arbitrary. We shall search in
vain for Melbury's homestead; for the cottage that
sheltered Marty South; for the house where Fitzpiers
lived; for the home of Giles Winterborne. Time
has done its work too thoroughly in this direction.
The woodlands themselves have altered in appearance;
the full-grown timber-tree of to-day was a mere sapling
at the time the story was written; what was mature
timber then has long been converted into planks, and
distributed hither and thither; some of the old plantations have been rooted and transformed into agricultural land, while new plantations have sprung up as
substitutes. But, in spite of these many changes, we

85.—A Saw-Pit near Middlemarsh.

86.—Woodlands near Minterne.

can still allow our imaginations rein when we stand among the woodlands to-day and gaze at the mature oaks, or the sapling beeches, or the struggling seedlings; and for the moment we may lose count of time and mentally reconstruct the scenes in which figured the familiar forms of Melbury, and Grace, and Marty South, and Winterborne, as they played their allotted parts (86).

We may spend many pleasant days in the country of "The Woodlanders," rambling here and there, journeying from village to village, taking the footpaths in preference to the roads, trying to conjecture where this or that incident was supposed to have taken place; or walking along the ridge of High-Stoy, whence we may catch an occasional glimpse between the trees of a house or church or farmstead; while beyond the woodlands which spread themselves out at our feet we can see far into the "Vale of the White Hart," and even can catch a glint of the waters of the Bristol Channel. In precisely the opposite direction spreads the distant Solent.

The scenery on which the curtain rises displays a spot on the high road leading from *Sherton Abbas* to *Abbot's Cernel.* The former of these places is virtually Sherborne; the latter Cerne Abbas. At this particular point on the highway Barber Percomb stops to inquire his way to *Little Hintock.* If we follow the directions which are given him we shall come to the hamlet of Hermitage. High-Stoy Hill had been visible to him for some miles back on the road he had travelled (87). It rears itself out of the valley on our right hand as we face Minterne—Dogbury Hill being on our left hand—and forms a landmark visible, and easily recognised, from long distances, a fact owing partly to its shape and partly to its altitude (88). The hill commands an extensive view over the vale below, and we shall have occasion to refer to it repeatedly in following the course of "The Woodlanders'" history. The serpentine road which ascends out of Lion's Gate village is the same as that

87.—HIGH-STOY.

88.—VIEW FROM HIGH-STOY, LOOKING TOWARDS DOGBURY HILL.

III

which Fitzpiers and Grace are supposed to have climbed when the former was on his way to visit Mrs. Charmond at *Middleton Abbey*. After they parted, Grace "ascended the slope of High-Stoy and watched his descent (89). . . . His way was east. . . ." The same two characters come before us again at the summit of this hill when, after their separation, Fitzpiers begs Grace to grant him an interview.

The actual house which formed the model for *Great Hintock House*, and which was supposed to have stood at no great distance from *Little Hintock*, has been swept away since the date at which the characters were imagined to have lived. It has been stated that the house had a reality in Upcerne House —a delightful Tudor mansion standing on the south side of Batcombe Down—but although certain features in the description may have been taken from this house, we cannot consider it typical, either in regard to its architecture or its situation.

The church, with the adjoining graveyard in which Giles Winterborne was supposedly interred, was a composite structure, drawn in part from the church of Melbury Bubb, as well as from that of Hermitage— which more nearly represents its position (90).

Some details certainly suggest Middlemarsh. Here we are concerned in a search for *Revellers Inn*, whither Tim and Suke and the wedding party were bound when Fitzpiers met them. "Just walking round the parishes to show ourselves a bit," was their explanation to him. This inn was once a posting-house of no mean size, but is now a farm-house and passes by the name of Revels Farm (91). It is an old building and possesses certain suggestive features reminding us of its former employment. In what was once the bar we may see the money-till underneath a bench-table with a well-worn slot in it, through which the coins were dropped. Connecting the bar-room with the old kitchen is a glass door with curious latticed panes of bottle-glass.

89.—VIEW FROM HIGH-STOY.

90.—HERMITAGE CHURCH.

We will now glance at the places outside the boundary of the *Hintock* country. *Middleton Abbey* is mentioned as the temporary residence of Mrs. Charmond. The abbey at Milton Abbas seems to have suggested it to our author. We find an interesting village, built on model lines; all the houses on both sides of the long wide street are almost exactly similar in size and design, and all are roofed with thatch. There used to be a magnificent avenue of chestnut trees, but these were pollarded a year or two ago because of the dampness caused by their over-hanging branches; they are beginning to recover themselves, however, and in a few years we may again see the grand display of blossom which made the village so conspicuous. The fine old abbey, which gives the place part of its name, comes as a sudden surprise to the traveller, for among the quiet rural surroundings we little expect to see this ancient building of Saxon foundation (92). Close beside the abbey-church stands the house which was doubtless imagined as the place of Mrs. Charmond's sojourn.

The village of *Oakbury Fitzpiers*, which Melbury pointed out to Grace as being the ancient home of the Fitzpiers family, seems to us to be represented in Okeford Fitzpaine, a village lying in the valley of the Stour in the direction of Blandford—a town which appears more or less identical with the *Shottsford-Forum* of the story.

Sherton Abbas, the fascinating old town full of quaint bits of architecture and mediæval buildings, comes before us as an approximation of Sherborne. The market-place, right in the centre of the town, is where we picture Giles Winterborne standing under his specimen apple-tree, close to the sixteenth-century conduit, which was placed there after its removal from the cloisters of the abbey (93). The Digby Hotel seems to answer to the "Earl of Wessex"; but the "Three Tuns," a hostel of much less importance, must have been drawn from one of the many inns which have

91.—REVELS FARM.

92.—MILTON ABBEY.

disappeared of late years. A visit to the abbey-church will bring back to us the day when Grace and Giles went there, "walked about the abbey aisles and presently sat down." The abbey-church displays to us many distinct periods in its architecture—Norman, Early English, Decorated, and Perpendicular. From the year 705 to 1075 Sherborne was the seat of a

93.—THE MARKET PLACE, SHERBORNE.

bishopric which included Dorset, Somerset, and part of Wilts and Devon.

Sherborne is a delightfully situated old-world town, surrounded by high hills from which we may see some panoramic views of the neighbourhood that include many landscapes interesting to the Hardy reader. On market days the little town is very busy and the streets are crowded; but on other days it exhibits an attitude towards strangers which can only be termed "sleepy." Among the many interesting buildings is the school; in the museum attached to it we shall find

the noted megalosaurus, whose upper and lower jaws
are more perfect than any other specimen extant.
With the old castle we shall deal later, when it serves
as the background for "Anna Lady Baxby," in "A
Group of Noble Dames."

The final scene takes us back to the churchyard
of *Little Hintock* and "a motionless figure standing
by the gate." Marty South is pictured visiting the
grave of Giles Winterborne. But there is no stone
marking the spot, no clue to guide us in our search,
and we must leave the country of "The Woodlanders"
with the frank admission that we have not discovered
as much as we could wish.

CHAPTER VII

"UNDER THE GREENWOOD TREE, OR THE
MELLSTOCK QUIRE"

THIS story deals with a phase of rural life which is now unfortunately extinct. A quarter of a century ago a string-choir might still be heard occasionally in some of the village churches in Wessex, but the only instances to-day are where certain vicars have endeavoured to revive the string-music for some special service—a proceeding which has not always proved to be the success anticipated. In the preface to the last edition of this novel we find some interesting details about the players: "Their music in those days was all in their own manuscript, copied in the evenings after work, and their music-books were home-bound." Some of the instruments were actually made by the players themselves. Here are facts which show us how strong was the interest taken in their work by the musicians: they had then a prescriptive interest in the services; the instruments and the music-books were handed down from father to son through many generations. Whilst earnestly determined to do their duty to the church in which they performed, they nevertheless found ample leisure to play tricks on one another. There is an authentic story told of two brothers, one of whom accused the other of "blowin' too harrd an' dhrownin' t'others' instruments." But as the recipient of the accusation stoutly denied the imputation, and refused to moderate his vigorous

94.—A Manuscript Music-Book.

95.—Bockhampton Cross Roads.

performance, the brother packed his flute with paper in such a manner as to leave only one note open, and the player, blissfully unconscious, continued to follow the score with unabated zeal!

The present writer has seen and handled some of the home-made instruments, as well as several of the manuscript music-books. The latter often contain a curious mixture of carols, secular songs, psalms, and quaint ditties more suitable to Christmas revelry than church worship. The accompanying illustration is reproduced from a manuscript music-book which once belonged to a noted member of the *Mellstock Quire*[1] (94). It may not be necessary to remind readers that, until the end of the seventeenth century, this word was written as pronounced, viz. Quire, a spelling still retained in the Book of Common Prayer. The story is laid in or about the year 1840—a date at which the " ecclesiastical bandsmen " played in many churches in the neighbourhood of *Mellstock*.

In tracing the backgrounds which figure in this book we find ourselves concerned with localities rather than with buildings, for with few exceptions these have been swept away or so completely altered as to render recognition impossible. The fictitious name of *Mellstock* included the several villages, hamlets, and isolated houses comprised in the parish of Stinsford. Upper and Lower Bockhampton, Stinsford House and cottages, Kingston Maurward, Bhompston, and Higher Kingston may all be regarded as suggestively comprehended in the general name.

Mellstock Lane is the road leading northwards from *Mellstock Cross*—the right-angled roads which intersect about two miles from Dorchester on the Tincleton road (95). Here we are introduced to the members of the choir, who are supposed to be on their way to Dick Dewy's house at *Upper Mellstock* —a place which seems to us to be typical of Upper

---

[1] The circular mark on the right-hand page is a stain resulting from the wet base of a cider mug.

96.—UPPER BOCKHAMPTON.

97.—THE BRIDGE AND RIVERSIDE HOUSE, LOWER BOCKHAMPTON.

Bockhampton (96). As they journey thither they soon see "glimmering indications of the few cottages forming the small hamlet." If we are correct in our surmise, we shall easily find the little hamlet; the tranter's house, however, has disappeared. It was a composite picture, drawn from two models, one of which is no longer in existence, while the other has been so much altered as to show no resemblance to "the long low cottage with a hipped roof of thatch" familiarised to us in the story.

If we follow the choir when, having first refreshed themselves with the tranter's cider—made probably from a purely local apple, the "Bock'a'ton Sweet" (Bock'a'ton being a corruption of Bockhampton),—they make a start for the "outlying homesteads and hamlets," we are led to the school-house at *Lower Mellstock*—a place approximating closely to Lower Bockhampton. The present school-house may have been built since the date of the story, though it bears no great unlikeness to the building from which the *Mellstock* school-house was drawn.

The next house to be visited is Farmer Shiner's, and we may discover its prototype in the house standing above the bridge at the bottom of the village, nowadays more enclosed than formerly (97).

We now see them crossing *Mellstock Bridge* and going along "an embowered path beside the Froom" on their way to the church and vicarage. The pathway interests us more particularly as one of the features in the mystic poem entitled "The Dead Quire." As we pass along it we catch a glimpse through the trees of the *Knapwater House* which figures in "Desperate Remedies." The call at the vicarage—suggested by the house standing close to Stinsford Church (98)—is the last for that night, and the respective members of the choir soon disperse and go homewards.

The next scene is supposed to take place in *Mellstock*—presumably Stinsford Church. This church

98.—Stinsford Vicarage.

99.—The Church Gate, Stinsford.

has been twice restored of late years and the old musicians' gallery removed. It contains some interesting monuments to the Pitt family, also a brass tablet to the memory of some Hardys of our author's family who are buried here. The piers of the "north gate or 'church hatch'" are crowned with two large decorated urns (99). It is with the old gallery that we are particularly concerned. It had "a status and sentiment of its own," we are told ; and we can readily credit the relative ecclesiastical grades of those who occupied it and those who sat in the body of the church. "The nave knew nothing of the gallery people, as gallery people, beyond their loud-sounding minims and chest notes."

The workshop of Mr. Penny stood, we are told, in "the lower village." We cannot trace such a place there now, but from one of the older residents we can hear of just such a workshop having been there long ago, and we have seen a water-colour of the same.

Yellowham Wood, in its imaginary name of *Yalbury Wood*, is the background for the scene when Dick goes, with "Smart the mare and the light spring-cart," to fetch Fancy from her father's house. This wood figures several times in the Novels and in the Poems. It is about half-way between Dorchester and Puddletown. The keeper's cottage—now remodelled—which was imagined as her home, lies a little off the road ; it is reached by a drove turning off just at the bottom of the hill on the Dorchester side (100). Its principal feature in our author's mind seems to have been the huge "chimney-corner"—for which we shall, however, look in vain. Its original size may be surmised from the information given us that it was large enough to contain, "in addition to Geoffrey himself, Geoffrey's wife, her chair, and her work-table, entirely within the line of the mantel, without danger or even inconvenience from the heat of the fire." Occasional instances of these cavernous chimney-corners, quite

100.—THE KEEPER'S COTTAGE, YELLOWHAM WOOD.

101.—THE SHIP INN, UPWEY.

common in our author's youth, are to be met with still, but they become rarer year by year.

The action now turns for a short time to *Budmouth*—the name under which Weymouth passes in the Wessex Novels. It forms an important stage for some scenes in "The Dynasts," and occurs frequently in "The Trumpet-Major." Dick is assumed to have gone there with some swarms of bees for Mr. Maybold's mother and to have met Fancy at "the corner of Mary Street . . . near the King's statue." We see them in imagination as they drive homewards together to *Mellstock*. The road passes through Upwey, and just at the foot of Ridgeway Hill stands the inn called "The Ship," where we are told they stopped to have tea and rest the horse (101). This appears to have been a momentous tea-drinking, for by and by "the newly-affianced youth and maiden passed up the steep hill to the Ridgeway, and vanished in the direction of *Mellstock*."

At the highest point in Upper Bockhampton, just where *Egdon Heath* commences, there is a wood on the left-hand side through which a drive has been cut. If we follow this track it will bring us out into the high road leading from Dorchester to Puddletown. Just opposite is another gate, giving into a further section of the same wood, and in which a similar pathway will be found. This we may recognise as the "Snail-Creep"—still its name—the path followed by Dick when he went nutting in Grey's Wood (102). He had reached it by way of Cuckoo Lane—the northern section of the track known in this novel as *Mellstock Lane*. As he is returning homewards, and just as he has "passed over a ridge which rose keenly against the sky," he comes up with Fancy. We can track them step by step as they proceed towards the school-house.

A little later in the narrative we see the vicar going towards *Casterbridge*—already stated to be an approximation to Dorchester; he falls in with Dick

102.—THE PATH INTO GREY'S WOOD.

103.—YELLOWHAM HILL.

THE WESSEX OF THOMAS HARDY

and walks beside him until they reach Grey's Bridge. Dick leaves him to go to *Durnover Mill* (Fordington Mill); but "Mr. Maybold leant over the parapet of the bridge and looked into the river." He had just heard from Dick of his engagement to Fancy, and his heart was heavy. This bridge has often served our author as the supposed resting-place of those whose minds were perturbed — Michael Henchard, in "The Mayor of Casterbridge," and other familiar characters.

We have already discovered the cottage in *Yalbury Wood*, and we turn thither again for the final scene. It is the day of the wedding, and many old friends are gathered there. We see them starting for the church—"every man to his maid. . . . Now among dark perpendicular firs . . . now through a hazel copse . . . now under broad beeches in bright young leaves they threaded their way into the high road over *Yalbury Hill*, which dipped at that point directly into the village of Fancy's parish" (103). No name is given, but we may take it for granted that the reference is to *Weatherbury*—pictured from the Puddletown of long ago—which we have visited in a previous chapter.

CHAPTER VIII

"LIFE'S LITTLE IRONIES" AND "A FEW CRUSTED CHARACTERS"

An Imaginative Woman

WE may regard Southsea as being in our author's mind when he took *Solentsea* as the background for this story, but we find no clue to help us in identifying the particular house in which the Marchmonts were supposed to have lodged. Southsea is essentially a seaside resort and forms the residential quarter of Portsmouth. To the archæologist there is little of interest attaching to the town; the castle, built by Henry VIII., stands at the southern extremity of Portsea Island. Just opposite the sea-front, and only separated from the mainland by the inlet of the English Channel, lies the Isle of Wight; doubtless this is the spot designated by our author as the "Island opposite."

If Southsea is lacking in interest, the island fully compensates for the deficiency in its high cliffs and sheltered bays, deep-wooded depressions and bare downs to the height of 700 feet above the sea.

The undercliff is a terrace of natural construction, sheltered by precipices above and behind, and offers a home to many delicate plants. On the south side of the island are the famous ravines, cut through the soft rock by the action of rivulets, mimicking the cañons of the far west where full-fed rivers rush along. The Needles, originally four in number, lie off the westernmost point; during a storm in 1764 one of the spires was undermined and fell; their chief constituent is chalk, and they are about 100 feet in height. Alum Bay is perhaps the most interesting spot to the geologist, for here the vertical disposition of the strata is very clearly defined; many fossils are to be met with, and at Brook Point there exists an extensive fossil forest.

THE SON'S VETO

"In a remote nook in North Wessex, forty miles from London, near the thriving town of Aldbrickham (Reading), there stood a pretty village with its church and parsonage. . . ." This introduces us to the village called *Gaymead*, and we may identify it more or less closely with Shinfield, a hamlet standing a little distance off the main road from Reading to Basingstoke, and about four miles from the former. It is certainly a pretty village; many of the houses are of half-timber construction and are overhung with trees. The church is a fine example of flint-work and has a square, solid-looking brick tower with battlemented parapets and handsome string courses (104). It was originally built in the thirteenth century; the tower is later, perhaps sixteenth century. Inside are a number of interesting monuments, and the roof is of massive timbers, curiously strutted. This is the church wherein we picture the marriage of Sophy and the rector; and in the churchyard Sophy was supposedly laid to rest. The vicarage is near by, but it is a comparatively new building devoid of any particular interest (105)

A London suburb is the next background; it, however, bears no distinctive features by which we can distinguish it among two or three on the south side, though the Clapham Road would meet the description. Sophy is residing here after her widowhood, and one day she sees Sam passing along the road in the early morning with a load of vegetables for Covent

104.—SHINFIELD·CHURCH.

105.—SHINFIELD VICARAGE.

Garden Market—a scene that may be witnessed any early morning in the suburbs of London. Soon after her ride beside him we are told that he takes a fruiterer's business in *Aldbrickham*—a town cast in the semblance of Reading. We can scarcely hope to pick out the actual shop after this lapse of time, and the only clue we are given regarding it is that it was the largest of its kind in the town. In our mind's eye we can see Sam standing at the door some four years later watching a funeral procession as "it passed his door and went out of the town towards the village of Gaymead."

FOR CONSCIENCE' SAKE

From the story told by Millborne we learn that he "came up to town at one-and-twenty, from Toneborough, in Outer Wessex." *Toneborough* is our author's imaginative Taunton; the fact that it stands on the river Tone suggests to us the origin of its fictitious name, and, if we remember rightly, this tale is the first to introduce it into these chronicles. In mediæval times the fairs—now held twice yearly—were celebrated for the sale of a woollen cloth called "Tauntons." The parish church is one of the largest and finest in the country. There are some relics of Norman work; Early English is represented in the north aisles and transepts; but the main building is Perpendicular (106). The castle, now used as a museum, and containing some interesting prehistoric and other antiquities, was largely rebuilt in 1496, but its original date was much earlier than this, the walls and the keep being twelfth century.

It was here that the ill-fated meeting of Millborne and Leonora was supposed to take place; but when later he wished to marry her it was to *Exonbury* he had to go in order to find her. Exeter is more or less the prototype of *Exonbury*; no particular spot is mentioned here except the house in which Leonora

106.—THE PARISH CHURCH, TAUNTON.

107.—WELLS.

133

lived, and which cannot now be accurately determined. After a passing reference to London, and again to the Isle of Wight, the action turns to *Ivell*. In Anglo-Saxon times Yeovil was known as Evill or Ivle, and the local pronunciation to-day is Iv'll; this suffices to tell us the town figured in our author's mind as *Ivell*. Cope is represented as the curate of St. John's Church —a Perpendicular building of cruciform shape containing some fine windows of that style, and interesting brasses of the fifteenth and sixteenth centuries. Under the chancel is a thirteenth-century crypt. It is here that the Millbornes eventually come to reside, living in a "little old manor-house . . . standing a mile from Mr. Cope's town of Ivell."

A Tragedy of Two Ambitions

The action of this story is also laid in and around Yeovil. With the prologue we have little to do; the village is not mentioned by name, and is only referred to as being in a distant county. Wells, in its guise of *Fountall*, comes before us for a time (107), the Cathedral Close receiving frequent mention; in it we see the elder Halborough stand, "staring quizzically at the west front of the cathedral." This now old-fashioned city of Wells, lying in a hollow under the Mendip Hills, amid beautiful scenery, was one of the most important towns of Wessex in Saxon times. The 600 figures on the west front of its cathedral, most of them life-size or larger, represent kings and queens of Saxon, Norman, and Plantagenet times, as well as many angels, prophets, and saints.

Thence the action moves to *Narrobourne*, strongly suggestive of West Coker (108).

On the Western Circuit

The first background to this story we find in the market-square at *Melchester*—typical of Salisbury.

108.—West Coker.

109.—The Cathedral Close, Salisbury.

135

The fair is in full swing, and we picture Raye leaving his quiet contemplation of the cathedral—the "most homogeneous pile of mediæval architecture in England" (109)—and entering the turmoil in the market-place. *Melchester* has already received our consideration in previous chapters, but the house imagined to be the home of the Harmans is a fresh object to us. It was "a dignified residence of considerable size," and it gave on to the square. A building answering to the description, though not now a private residence, may be found near the north-east corner.

Our next exploration will be "the earthworks of Old Melchester," where Raye takes Anna for a walk (110). The associations of Old Sarum are profoundly inter-esting to the archæologist; the huge mound is hollowed out in the centre like a crater, and the rim is topped by a rampart; it descends almost sheerly to a depth of one hundred feet. It was a stronghold of the early Britons. To the Romans it was known as *Sor-biodunum*. Early in the sixth century it was the seat of Cerdic, founder of the Wessex Kingdom. In the reign of Edward the Confessor it possessed a mint. In 1075 it became the seat of a bishopric, transferred thither from Sherborne. On the "Sarum Breviary," printed in Venice in 1483, was based the prayer-books of Edward VI. It was not until the thirteenth century that the new city of Salisbury sprang into existence; but the walls of the old city remained standing until early in the seventeenth century, when they were demolished. According to Ptolemy (second century) Sarum was a place of Celtic origin.

The "Great Mid-Wessex Plain" is obviously suggestive of Salisbury Plain, and it was in one of the villages lying within its boundaries that Anna was brought up—the same place in which Edith Harman had passed her early life. The actual position of this village we cannot determine, though it seems not far from Stonehenge. Unfortunately, much of the poetry of the *Great Plain* has disappeared within recent years,

110.—OLD SARUM (SALISBURY).

111.—POOLE.

owing to the advent of military camps, an innovation which will appeal less to the æsthetic than to the utilitarian section of English people. This vast expanse of green downland, only occasionally broken by cultivated stretches, used to convey a sense of loneliness and remoteness from civilisation that impressed the visitor with a peculiar feeling of delight; one might wander mile after mile without meeting a single human being, and the only evidence of sentient life was to be looked for in the flocks of sheep grazing here and there, or a distant glimpse of a shepherd with his dog. But to-day that is all changed; the contours of the grassy undulations are marred by military tents or groups of temporary structures; and instead of a distant call from a shepherd to his dog, our ears are met by frequent bugle-calls.

The action turns to London, and there the marriage of our two chief characters takes place. The last we see of them is as they speed along in the train, bound for *Knollsea*, the fictitious presentment of Swanage.

To Please his Wife

Poole, the town which approximates to the *Havenpool* of the Wessex Novels, forms the background in this story (111). It is built on a peninsula formed by the waters of Poole Harbour, an irregular, many-bayed inlet, and, on the other side, by Holes Bay. The harbour, with its exceedingly narrow mouth, extends nearly six miles inland, and has an average breadth of about four miles. Of the many islands which are dotted about, Branksea, or Brownsea, is the largest; on it is a castellated residence, once a castle of defence, built in the Tudor period as a safeguard for the harbour. It is a picturesque sheet of water, but by no means easy to navigate, for the ebb of the tide leaves only narrow channels, difficult to follow except to those who are really familiar with its intricacies. When viewed from the height of Nine-Barrow Down on the south, or from Lytchett Beacon on the north, the wide stretch of water, with its islands cropping up here and there, has a lake-like appearance, and has earned for itself the title of "The Dorset Lakes." At the mouth of the estuary are the Sandbanks, a low-lying stretch of loose sand which would without doubt have dissolved and filled up the channel had protecting groynes not been built to break the force of the sea. There is a double tide in the harbour; after flowing for six hours it ebbs for an hour and a half, and then flows again for the same period, thus making a second high-water, and ebbs again for the remaining three hours.

Although there are numerous barrows and British earthworks scattered about the environs of Poole, and traces exist of a Roman road leading from there to Wimborne, we possess no very early chronicles of the town. It is first mentioned historically in 1224, when "the bailiffs and good men of La Pole" were ordered to retain all ships within their port.

We are introduced to Joliffe when he is imagined as entering St. James' Church to offer up a thanksgiving for his deliverance from shipwreck. This is the parish church, erected in 1820 on the site of an ancient building. In the High Street we are also interested; it is the main thoroughfare which bisects the town and leads down to the quay. The quay is one of the most interesting parts of the town, for here forgather men of many nationalities; it also serves as a sort of club-lounge for the loafers of the town and the gossips (112). To the wharves come many foreign ships, laden chiefly with timber; and from here is shipped a considerable amount of the clay for which the district is famous. Close beside the quay we find the old town cellars, exhibiting the most ancient building in Poole, dating from the reign of Edward III. Looking on to the High Street is a Georgian house, now used as a hospital, and we have every reason to think this was appropriated by our author as a model for "the worthy merchant's home, one of those large substantial brick mansions frequently jammed up in old-fashioned towns."

In imagination we can picture Joanna climbing the toilsome ascent of Constitution Hill, "whence a view of the open channel could be obtained," to gaze seawards in the hope of seeing her husband's ship return. From the apex of this hill a magnificently wide view stretches before us: the harbour, broken by the many islands and inlets; the Purbeck Hills behind forming the ultimate background, with the jagged walls of Corfe Castle standing out against them; while to the eastward we can note the narrow neck of the harbour, leading into the English Channel.

THE FIDDLER OF THE REELS

When we were examining the sites and scenes in "Under the Greenwood Tree" we recognised, close to the bridge at Lower Bockhampton, a long low house which was supposed to represent the home of Farmer Shiner. The same place comes before us now as the house at which Wat Ollamoor lodged. We hear of Car'line Aspent pausing on this bridge and becoming fascinated by the fiddler's music. At that time she was dwelling with her father, the parish clerk, who lived in the middle of the village of *Stickleford*. Tincleton has already done duty for *Stickleford*; there are two distinct clusters of houses here, and we are inclined to locate the clerk's house in the more western, and older, cluster, near to the farm-house which we decided to regard as the model for Venn's dairy-house in "The Return of the Native" (113).

The action turns for a time to London, but again reverts to South Wessex. We may picture the Hipcrofts journeying to *Casterbridge* (Dorchester) by rail, and Car'line and the child setting out to walk to *Stickleford*. At "a certain half-way house, widely known as an inn," they were to await the arrival of Ned. Here, at the inn familiarised to us as *The Quiet*

112.—THE QUAY, POOLE.

113.—TINCLETON VILLAGE.

Woman, the mother and child find Mop Ollamoor, and when Ned comes on the scene it is to discover that Mop has disappeared and taken the little girl with him. We may picture the fancied pursuit across *Egdon*. " Outside the house, on the other side of the highway, a mass of dark heath-land rose sullenly upward to its not easily accessible interior, a ravined plateau, whereon jutted into the sky . . . the fir-woods of Mistover, backed by the Yalbury coppices." This description of the scene is true to-day, excepting that the *Mistover* fir-woods have passed out of existence, burnt in some of the fires which have ravaged the heath. This section of South Wessex is very familiar to those of us who have visited the home of Eustacia Vye, and it would seem needless to describe it further here.

" A Few Crusted Characters "

If we enter Dorchester by the London Road we shall see, on our right hand, just at the commencement of the town, an inn bearing the name of the White Hart, a fine wooden specimen of that animal gracing the top of the porch. On any market day we may find the yard in front of the inn thronged with carriers' vans, all typical of the particular van mentioned in the short tales we are examining. " Burthen, Carrier to Longpuddle," is the title it bears, and in *Long-puddle* we shall recognise a strong resemblance to the villages of Pydelhinton and Pydeltrenthide, the apt naming of the fictitious place striking us at once as we explore the two long straggling villages which are practically connected to each other.

Let us follow Burthen's van as it starts from the White Hart. First come the open meadows — the *Durnover Moor* of the Wessex Novels—Grey's Bridge occurring about midway ; then, taking the left-hand road, we climb Waterstone, or Climmerstone Ridge— scene of the poem entitled " The Revisitation "—by

114.—Pydelhinton Church.

115.—Frampton Church.

way of Slyre's Lane, which brings us to the summit by
a series of rises and dips.   Once at the top of the hill,
the road descends into the valley of the Pydele and
follows that little stream upwards, the road running
parallel with the river.   According to local repute, the
district is one wherein a man can "neither live nor
die"—which means it is too poor for him to make a
living in, while the climate is too healthy to allow him
to perish!   It was on this road that Tony got himself
into the pickle he himself describes as a "nunny-
watch."

"The History of the Hardcomes" has *Budmouth-
Regis* as its background, a place well known to us as
semblable to Weymouth.   "They looked at the ships
in the harbour," we read, "and then went up to the
Look-out," which is now called the Nothe.

In "The Superstitious Man's Story" we are interested in a matter outside the scope of mere topography.   The church is not mentioned by name, but
the inference points to it being the church of *Longpuddle*—which we are led to perceive as that of Pydelhinton (114).   William Privett's midnight visit to the
church porch brings before us a custom or superstition
still believed in by some of the older people in the less
sophisticated parts of Wessex, and the present writer
has met several people who firmly believed in the
custom, and who, according to their own showing, had
proved its outcome to be true.

The story of "Andrey Satchel and the Parson and
Clerk" has its action at *Scrimpton*, a village nearly
identical with Frampton, or Frome-town.   Here, in the
beautiful old church built in the fifteenth century, the
wedding is imagined to have taken place (115).   There
was once a Benedictine priory at Frampton, and close to
the village is the site of an ancient British settlement.

The story called "Absent-mindedness in a Parish
Choir" brings back to us the novel entitled "Under the
Greenwood Tree," where we find many interesting
details relating to the "ecclesiastical bandsmen."   The

episode is supposed to have taken place in the gallery of *Longpuddle* Church, already referred to as Pydelhinton.

"The Winters and the Palmleys" takes us into *Yalbury Wood*. There used to be a curious superstition current with regard to Yellowham Wood. It was said to be the haunt of a mysterious personage known as "The Wild Man o' Yall'm," to whom was attributed the paternity of many of the "love-children" in the neighbouring villages. He was also credited with causing many unpleasant surprises to those belated souls who chanced to find themselves under the shade of the Yellowham trees after nightfall. There is an unimpeachable story of a girl who was arraigned before the local magistrates, and who, in reply to a question as to the paternity of her child, replied : "Please your Worshipfuls, 'twer' the Wild Man o' Yall'm."

To find the field of action for the "Incident in the Life of Mr. George Crookhill" we must explore the northern portion of South Wessex. "Georgy was ambling out of Melchester" and overtook a "fine-looking young farmer" near Bissett Hill. This hill is about three miles from Salisbury on the road leading through Blandford to Dorchester. At Woodyates Inn—occurring under its present-day name and easily discovered—they stopped to bait their horses ; at *Trantridge*—a place akin to Pentridge—they passed the night. At East Woodyates the road intersects the old Roman Road, or Via Iceniana, which runs in a straight line to Badbury Rings. *Vindogladia*, the Roman Station, is regarded by some authorities to have been synonymous with Woodyates. The by-lane down which they are supposed to have ridden would no doubt be this same Roman Road.

We read that "the figure of Mr. Lackland was seen at the inn, and in the village street, and in the fields and lanes about Upper Longpuddle," the designation "Upper" seeming to denote Pydeltrenthide.

CHAPTER IX

"WESSEX TALES"

THE THREE STRANGERS

THIS very popular story, both in narrative and as a play, has for its scenery a locality which seems particularly appropriate. If we journey to Grimstone and take our way up Long Ash Lane, the old Roman Road which led from Dorchester to Yeovil, we shall note on our right hand a wind-swept, desolate country which seems to echo the voices we hear in imagination coming from the cottage standing on "the solitary hill of Higher Crowstairs." It is all very forlorn, very sombre ; strangers are rarely seen here, and only those frequent the downs whose work lies thereon. From the top of the downs a wide view of the surrounding country can be had. To the south-east lies Dorchester, hedged in by its avenues of trees ; behind it Bincombe Down and the Ridgeway shut out the sea.

It is to the lonely habitation here that the three strangers are imagined to come. The first to arrive is the escaped prisoner from *Casterbridge* Gaol ; the second is the hangman, passing on his way to the very place the other had come from ; the third had tramped from *Shottsford*, a town symbolical of Blandford. We may readily picture the hurried exit of the third stranger and his subsequent pursuit by the rest of the party, armed with lanterns and hurdle-staves ; and in imagination we watch them scrambling over the downs, falling down the lynchets, and eventually returning with the innocent man in custody.

A Tradition of 1804

Solomon Selby's tale of the "Corsican Tyrant" takes us to Lulworth Cove and the downs that surround it, for we have already pictured Lulworth as approximately identical with *Lulstead* or *Lulwind*. "Uncle Job" is supposed to have been in camp "on the downs above King George's watering-place"— evidently Bincombe Down—and he comes to visit Solomon's father, and goes with the lad at night to look to the sheep. The cottage where Solomon lived is no longer discoverable, and our greed for topographical accuracy must be satisfied with a ramble on the downs above Lulworth Cove and a glance down into the Cove itself. To the geologist the cliffs here will prove particularly attractive on account of the different strata to be observed; while the undulating downs, covered with numerous barrows and some prehistoric earthworks, will delight all who are interested in archæology.

The Melancholy Hussar of the German Legion

This story is laid on a basis of historical fact, and we can afford to be definite in our identification of the backgrounds. Bincombe Down, soon to be familiar to us as a frequent scene in "The Trumpet-Major," and again to come before us when we explore the country connected with "The Dynasts," is the spot we are seeking (116). "Here stretch the downs, high and breezy and green, absolutely unchanged since those eventful days," says our author. The down overlooks one of the most extensive panoramas in the whole of the Wessex Country—"commanding the Isle of Portland in front, and reaching to St. Aldhelm's Head eastward and almost to the Start on the West."

The association of ancient days, of people who have long ago passed into dust, seems to linger around this grassy expanse, and we should think it difficult to conjure up a more fitting scene for the enactment of the tragedy which forms the *motif* of the story.

"The small, dilapidated, half farm half manor-house," in which Phyllis Grove is supposed to have lived, has now completely disappeared, leaving no tangible evidence of its existence. Only the church remains as an uninscribed monument to the two comrades (117). Their bodies lie in the graveyard attached, and the actual spot used to be pointed out by some of the older inhabitants; but there is no memorial tablet, and we must rely on the memory of those who have had the mounds indicated to them by their parents. In the parish register may still be seen the entries relating to the burial of the two deserters, under the date of June 30th, 1801. Men who saw them shot were known to living persons.

The plan of escape formulated by the Hussars seemed simple and promising for success. Phyllis was to meet her lover "at a point in the highway at which the lane to the village branched off," and, as we descend the Ridgeway Hill, we note a steep declivity on our left hand passing under the trees that edge the road and rising again to cross an open field. We recognise the spot at a glance. But for the miscarriage of their plans the lovers would then have made their way into Weymouth, would have crossed the harbour-bridge, climbed over the Nothe, and joined Christoph in the boat.

THE WITHERED ARM

We will take *Holmstoke* to be an approximate representation of East Stoke, a village on the Frome, three and a half miles west of Wareham. It is on the road from this place—the *Anglebury* of our author's imagining—that we see the farmer driving his wife

116.—BINCOMBE VILLAGE.

117.—BINCOMBE CHURCH.

home to "the white house of ample dimensions . . . with farm buildings and ricks at the back," the prototype of which is still to be found in the adjoining hamlet of West Holme (118).

The church mentioned in the story was drawn from the ruined aisles which are to be seen in the meadows at the back of the mill (119). Even at the period to which the story belongs it was spoken of as "an ancient little pile"; but in 1828 the new church was built— now on the other side of the railway constructed later, and close to the high road—since when only occasional services have been held in the decayed ruins.

The cottage which was supposed to shelter Rhoda Brook stood at "a lonely spot high above the water-meads and not far from the border of Egdon Heath." It has no particular description given to distinguish it from other similar cottages in the vicinity, but in any case we may assume that it has perished long ago. We may well conjecture where it stood, probably to the southward of the hamlet (120).

The story brings before us vividly one of the old-time superstitions which are now fast dying out. The dream which came to Rhoda is an incident by no means uncommon, and similar occurrences have been repeatedly brought before the writer of this Guide. By a certain class of people it would perhaps be referred to as a nightmare; amongst the less literate such a dreamer would describe herself as being "hag-rod," *i.e.* hag-ridden. Numberless cases could be quoted where such visitations have occurred, sometimes by day, but generally by night; and doubtless the recorded instances would be much more common, were it not that the sufferers are chary of mentioning the facts, save to those who will be more likely to show sympathy than scepticism.

The house in which Conjuror Trendle was supposed to live has fallen into complete decay; the walls were still standing twenty years ago, but we can only find the foundations now, and these are half hidden under

118.—HOLME FARM.

119.—THE RUINS OF THE OLD CHURCH, STOKE.

THE WESSEX OF THOMAS HARDY

a tangle of heather and brambles. Passing the spot
some years ago, the writer inquired of an old rustic
who was working near whether he remembered it
when it was occupied, and he replied that a man
used to live there who was "a seventh of a seventh,"
meaning a seventh son of a seventh son—a qualifica-
tion considered as a strict essential for the holding of
occult powers. These "conjurors," or (of the other
sex) "cunning women," or "white witches"—as they
were variously styled—once formed an important
section of rural communities, but they are seldom
heard of now.

We may picture Mrs. Lodge and Rhoda as they
"set out on their climb into the interior of this solemn
country," passing along the old highway which follows
the ridge separating the two valleys of the Froom and
the Pydel, and known as the Puddletown to Wareham
Road. We have passed along it before in imagination
when Diggory Venn came to Rainbarrow with his van
and the shaggy heath-croppers. From the ridge extends a magnificent view on both hands, and many
objects of interest to Hardy readers may be noted.
Straight before us is Clyffe Clump, standing this side
of the little village of *Stickleford*, with Rainbarrow
behind it. On our right hand, in the Pydel Vale, lie
the villages of *Kingsbere* and *East Egdon*, the former
backed by *Greenhill*—scene of the fair in "Far from
the Madding Crowd." On the left hand, in the Valley
of the Froom, lies *Holmstoke*, also *Wellbridge*, and in
the distance forming the horizon are the hills that shut
in *Lulstead Cove* and the country which forms the
landscapes in "The Distracted Preacher."

It is understood to be about six years later that
Gertrude visits the Conjuror for the second time, and
it is then that she learns how a cure may be brought
about. In consequence of this we see her riding
towards *Casterbridge* in order to reach the gaol.
"She did not take the direct road thither through
Stickleford (relatively Tincleton)," but rode by a

120.—HOLME BRIDGE.

121.—THE HANGMAN'S COTTAGE, DORCHESTER.

153

roundabout course until she entered the heath. When she at length reaches *Casterbridge* it is almost dark. At the entrance to the town stands that old hostelry the White Hart, a portion of which building overhangs the Froom, and here she stables her horse. We see her treading the path that runs beside the river— a path we have already traversed in the footsteps of Henchard—passing the old Priory Mill, and at length reaching the little thatched cottage which was her destination. It is called the Hangman's Cottage to this day (121). On the end wall may be traced the opening which formed the doorway to the upper room, which was reached by an outside flight of stairs.

On the following day we see her in our mind's eye undergoing the gruesome process known as "turning the blood," once credited by many people as an infallible cure for certain obscure diseases which defied medical diagnosis and treatment, and still believed in by some of the older generation of Wessex folk. We hear of Lodge returning home for a time, and then going to *Port Bredy*—a town we shall presently recognise as being drawn after the pattern of Bridport—where he ends his days.

FELLOW TOWNSMEN

The surroundings and scenery which figure in this story are to be found in and about the old-world town of Bridport, just alluded to in the previous story. *Port Bredy* bears the imprint of having once been a much larger and more important place; a ramble through the streets suggests at a glance that it has had a past, a history attaching to it of which its present guise gives but scant indication. This conjecture we find to be a true one; there is still a certain amount of commerce carried on within its boundaries, but only on a scale which is a mere echo of its former commercial importance.

It is recorded in Domesday Book that Bridport

possessed a mint and an ecclesiastical establishment.
Ropes, twines, fishing-nets, and the like, are still manu-
factured to some extent, but when Henry VIII. was
king it was prescribed by royal edict that all the
cordage used in the royal navy should be of Bridport
manufacture, its renown for ropes and cables dating
back to the early part of the thirteenth century. It
is interesting to note further that nearly all the flax
used for the purpose was grown in the vicinity.
Another production for which the town was famous
was that of hangmen's ropes; and out of this, which
was virtually a monopoly, arose the old saying that
So-and-so had been "stabbed with a Bridport dagger"
—a polite way of intimating that he had been hanged!
The town gets its name from the river Brid or Brit
which runs beside it and joins the Asker to flow into
the harbour at West Bay.

Let us regard Barnet and Downe as they are
imagined driving into the town—"past the little
town-hall, the Black Bull Hotel, and onward." We can
see the town-hall and the Bull Hotel which served as
models (122); the house in which Downe was supposed
to live was probably one of those still visible in the off-
street on the right, called Downe Street. The house
where Barnet resided has completely disappeared; the
site on which it stood, nearly opposite St. Mary's
Church, is now occupied by a chapel.

The town-hall was erected in 1786, and stands on
the site of the ancient Chapel of St. Andrew. The
Bull Hotel is a much older building; it was demised
by Daniel Taylor in the time of Charles II. to pay for
a schoolmaster to instruct the children of the town.
Château Ringdale may have been studied from a house
just out of the town on the western side encircled in
trees, but for the purposes of the story we must imagine
it placed near the road that leads to the harbour, now
West Bay.

St. Mary's Church was where Lucy Savile was
supposed to be married to Downe. There are some

122.—BRIDPORT.

123.—MELBURY OSMUND.

interesting monuments in this building, and a climb to the top of the tower will reward us with a fine view of the surrounding country.

If we now walk along the Harbour Road we shall pass the supposed site of *Château Ringdale* ; and just before we reach West Bay we may note on the right-hand side, standing a little back from the highway, a cottage which from its position seems to suggest the little house where Lucy lived. Continuing, we soon reach West Bay, the seaside suburb of Bridport, and see before us the "little haven, seemingly a beginning made by Nature herself of a perfect harbour."

INTERLOPERS AT THE KNAP

Long Ash Lane is still "a monotonous track without a village or hamlet for many miles, and with very seldom a turning." This is the old Roman Road which leads from Dorchester to Yeovil and is now seldom used, travellers preferring the lower and easier road which passes through Maiden Newton. Following the ancient highway, as did the three equestrians in the story, we shall in due course reach the forking roads at which they halted, a place we recognise as Holywell. We are informed that had they taken the left-hand road they would have come upon "an old house with mullioned windows of Ham-hill stone, and chimneys of lavish solidity. It stood at the top of a slope beside King's Hintock village street. . . ." *King's Hintock* is approximately Melbury Osmund, but the house, still remembered, has been demolished (123-124). Inside this house we await the arrival of Phillip and his wife. They had travelled through *Evershead* (Evershot), we are told, and he had looked in at the *Sow-and-Acorn*, an inn we perceive to be the " Acorn."

In this story is mentioned the curious custom of "telling the bees" after a death—a superstition still believed in by most of the inhabitants of rural Wessex ; the efficacy is supposed to be guaranteed if supple-

124.—MELBURY OSMUND.

125.—THE WHITE HORSE HOTEL, MAIDEN NEWTON.

mented by the affixing of a small piece of crape to each hive. A case came before the writer of these pages a few years ago where the survivors omitted to take this precaution, with the result that the bees, numbering fifty or more stocks, all died. Similar cases can be vouched for where the thing has happened.

The *White Horse* Inn at *Chalk-Newton* formed the half-way house between Darton's Farm and *King's Hintock*, and here Helena's boy is handed over to the care of Darton's bailiff. *Chalk-Newton* is more or less synonymous with Maiden Newton, and in the main street of this little town we find the inn mentioned (125). It was a fine old Elizabethan specimen of a hostelry, but was pulled down about twenty years ago. There is no clue given us by which we can discover the actual position of Darton's residence, but as it was twenty miles from *King's Hintock* we may safely conclude it lay at no great distance from Dorchester.

THE DISTRACTED PREACHER

It is the little village of Owermoigne, lying just off the road from Weymouth or Dorchester to Wareham, which is used under the assumed name of *Nether Moynton* as the background for this story. It was once the home of many a smuggler, and some of the old people living there now can remember taking part in smuggling enterprises ; but the reticence which in those days was essential to successful undertakings of this kind still lingers, and they prefer to clothe their reminiscences in the guise of "what father did say," or "what granfer twold I"—an allusion which we may safely conclude to be a veil—and only when they get thoroughly warmed up to their recitals does the impersonal note merge into the personal.

The village is only a short three miles from the coast, and is close to that portion of it which is shut in by high, unscalable cliffs, with sparsely populated downlands intervening. Thus we see how well situated it was as a home for such as delighted in defrauding the revenue—some by reason of the profits to be made, others from the love of excitement and adventure. Such episodes as the one described in our story were by no means uncommon in "the good old days," and many ingenious hiding-places are still in existence.

The Church of Owermoigne is a building in the Gothic style, but was rebuilt in 1883—a date subsequent to the story. Accordingly, we no longer find the "singing gallery stairs" where, under a pile of church debris, "decayed framework, pews, panels, and pieces of flooring," the barrels of illicit spirits were stored (126).

The house in which Lizzie Newberry was imagined to have lived was drawn from the house which stands almost opposite to the rectory (127); but the orchard belonging to her cousin Owlett does not quite adjoin her garden. It can, however, still be seen a little way off, and the remains of the artificial cave are perceptible as an irregularity in the ground.

Let us follow in the footsteps of Lizzie when she goes to the cliffs at night to take her part in the landing of the cargo. Leaving Owermoigne, we cross the high road and ascend the steep hill leading towards *Ringsworth* (Ringstead). At its summit we obtain a fine bird's-eye view of the country to the north, east, and west. Then we descend on the other side, and soon pass "the lonely hamlet of Holworth (figuring under its own name)," and soon after are in sight and sound of the sea.

We can imagine them crossing Chaldon Down, meeting the other members of the gang, and continuing till they reach "the crest of the hill at a lonely, trackless place not far from the ancient earthwork called Round Pond." If we glance at the ordnance map we shall be able to dog their footsteps over the undulating downs, crowned here and there with prehistoric barrows, and amid a wealth of scenery of exceeding diversity.

126.—Owermoigne Church.

127.—Owermoigne Village.

Nether Moynton is again the arena when the excisemen make their raid and at length discover the hiding-places of the smugglers, and then the action changes to *Warm'ell Cross* (Warmwell Cross)— the point where the roads to Weymouth and Dor-

128.—WARMWELL CROSS.

chester part (128). Here we see clumps of trees, and it does not require a very vivid imagination to picture the scene described, and to see in fancy the disappointed excisemen bound to the trees and shouting for help, a performance said to have been really enacted in the eighteen-thirties.

PART II

ROMANCES AND FANTASIES

CHAPTER I

"A PAIR OF BLUE EYES"

In order to discover the land- and sea-scapes from which the theatre of this story was drawn, we shall have to go to the most westerly portion of that great area familiar to us as Wessex. This particular tract concerns us only in this one book, and practically the whole of it is contained within a short radius of the quaint, sea-washed town of Boscastle. There are a few other scenes, it is true—in London, at Plymouth, and in spots still more remote ;—but those touched with local characterisation are within the area named.

Lest my readers should be disappointed later, it may be as well to state frankly at the outset that we shall have somewhat to readjust several of the features we are intent on discovering ere we can make them coincide with the artificial representations given us in the story. This was one of our author's earliest books, written forty or so years ago, and the alterations worked by time on the real spots, together with, perhaps, to a still greater extent the modifications due at the outset to imaginative treatment, account for any inaccuracy apparent in the scenes pictured when regarded as delineations of the actual ones we see to-day. But this applies only to certain architectural features and their positions ; the natural configurations are vividly realistic.

The tale has a unique interest in being the only one of the series in which the heroine is positively known to have been suggested by a real person.

165

Before commencing our researches we may glance for a moment at the general topography of the district.

The county of Cornwall possesses, as is well known, an individuality difficult to describe, but nevertheless very distinct. Within its boundaries is included a great dissimilarity of scenery. We have the romantic moorlands, broken up with the outcropping of gaunt jagged rocks, bare, desolate ; the seventy miles between Launceston and Mount's Bay has been described as "the dreariest strip of earth traversed by any English high road." Then we have the long valleys, flanked by grassy downs, many of them deep and narrow and densely wooded, through which the little rivers dance and jump from rock to rock and seldom follow a straight line for many yards together. On the coast we find three very distinct types of scenery : the dark, rugged slate cliffs; the serpentine rock with its marvellous colouring ; and the majestic, adamantine granite. This last is particularly seen in the neighbourhood of Land's End ; it crops out again in the Scilly Isles, said traditionally to have been once joined to the mainland, the submerged portion forming the ancient land called Lyonesse, and imagined to have contained 140 parish churches. Owing to the prevailing dampness and the heavy dews, the lower levels of the county displayed no extraordinary aridness in the late abnormally dry summer of 1911 ; the grass remained green, and growth appeared to be of the average, if not greater. On the west coast, as late as the end of October, many wild flowers might have been seen still in lusty bloom : gorse, heather, violets, blackberry blossom, and many others. Fuchsias here grow into trees, many of them blossoming high above the roofs of the cottages, while in the deep sheltered valleys the vegetation is luxuriant and extremely varied.

To return to that portion of the county with which we are most intimately concerned. At the time when the story commences the nearest railway station to *Endelstow* was *St. Launce's*—a name which easily sug-

gests Launceston to the least discerning reader (129).
But later a station was opened at *Camelton*—an
obvious representation of Camelford. To-day there
is another station still nearer, viz. Otterham. But
those who propose to make an examination of the
places to be presently described would find Boscastle

129.—LAUNCESTON.

the most convenient centre from which to explore.
If, however, we prefer to follow Stephen Smith as he
approaches *Endelstow* vicarage from *St. Launce's*, we
shall be at once struck with the realistic description
of the country from Launceston to the north coast
near Boscastle. To the present writer the following
details presented themselves with an almost uncanny

similitude : " Scarcely a solitary house or man had been visible along the whole dreary distance of open country. . . . The only lights apparent on earth were some spots of dull red, glowing here and there upon the distant hills . . . smouldering fires for the consumption of peat and gorse-roots."

130.—St. Juliot Rectory.

If we inquire our way and follow the lanes indicated, we shall be able to verify the hilly character given to this district : " They climbed a hill, then another hill piled on the summit of the first . . . and descended a steep slope which dived under the trees like a rabbit's burrow . . . and the chimneys and gables of the vicarage became darkly visible " (130).

There is ground for supposing that in describing this vicarage the writer had largely in his mind the rectory of St. Juliot. It is a much pleasanter journey thither than by the above route to take the footpath which leads us through the Vallency valley from Boscastle (131). In the autumn, when the trees are changing colour, the scenery is particularly enchanting. The valley is a deep one and very narrow ; close beside us on our right hand the little river takes its serpentine course, babbling fretfully over the rocks which form its bed ; sometimes there are still, quiet pools in which speckled trout may be discovered lurking close beside the stones ; in other spots it hurls itself down miniature cascades ; then for a time it flows in placid contentment. The hill on our right hand is clothed with dwarf trees, chiefly oaks, all leaning eastward with one accord, away from the prevailing winds, which have razed off their tops to a dead level, as though they had been trimmed by a pair of giant shears. The branches, sometimes to the topmost twigs, are shrouded in feathery grey lichen, testifying to the damp atmosphere which is so prevalent here. On our left hand the mountain is more broken, craggy rocks spring out here and there, and the intervening ground is covered with furze, rough grass, bracken, and stunted bushes.

As the path mounts gradually higher the stream gurgles some feet below us, and we soon catch a glimpse of the rectory of St. Juliot on our left hand, standing amidst a thick clump of trees, and a couple of fields away from the path. No actual details are given us in the narrative of the house itself, but from its position, apart from other reasons, we feel we are not very wide of the mark in claiming it as the model for *Endelstow Vicarage*.

From this observation point we can see the tower of the church a little distance ahead, and over the valley to the right we catch the pinnacled tower of another church—that of Lesnewth—of which more anon.

The church before us is the one we have cause

131.—The Vallency Valley.

132.—St. Juliot Church, Cornwall, before Restoration 1872.

to accept as the prototype of *West Endelstow*, a background to many important scenes. It is dedicated to St. Julietta, a martyr, respecting whom very little is known. In the churchyard is an ancient cross, once intended doubtless to fix a preaching-place; on the disc which surmounts the shaft is a boldly cut Maltese cross, or perhaps we should say a *patée*. The church is of the Perpendicular order of architecture, a type most usual throughout Cornwall. It is solidly built of granite-ashlar, and, like most Cornish churches, possesses very little ornamentation (132). It was restored in 1872, and a tablet of Sicilian marble on a ground of Carnsew granite has been recently erected in the north aisle to record the fact that the late Mrs. Thomas Hardy before her marriage laid the foundation-stone of the new portions, and conducted the music of the church while living at the rectory here with her sister and brother-in-law. Apart from this circumstantial evidence it has been generally understood for a long time that the personal appearance and even the character of Elfride were studied in some particulars from this lady as she showed herself in youth; though the other personages and the dramatic incidents of the story are quite fictitious.

But although we choose to recognise this as the church we are in search of, its position must not be accepted. From the description given in the story we must imagine it as standing on the other side of the rectory, nearer to the sea, and close to the summit of the hill. There is a point of view below us in the valley from where the church appears to stand more nearly to its supposed position (133); but even then we cannot bring it into proper focus with the rectory. We read of its environment: " Not a tree could exist up there: nothing but the monotonous grey-green grass "—a description which fixes it indubitably at the top of the hill in the full stroke of the west wind, and reveals to us that something of the situation has been borrowed from the site of Forrabury Church a couple of miles off. However, a stone stile gives access to the churchyard of St. Juliot, just as in our story. On one of the tombs may be seen this quaintly worded inscription :—

Her Raging disease Mock'd the powers of Medicine, and Snatch'd with Resistless Impetuosity an Indulgent Parent from her growing Offsprings.

Trebarwith Strand, which lies some five miles to the south of Boscastle, is by its very name suggestive of the *Barwith Strand* of the story, but there is no detailed description allotted to it. It was merely the object of an excursion, and for other than that has no particular claim to our notice here. " Barwith Strand . . . was duly visited. They then swept round by innumerable lanes, in which not twenty consecutive yards were either straight or level. . . ." This description of the roads—or rather lanes—of the locality is strongly borne out by personal experience. In passing along one of the old Roman roads the traveller very often becomes wearied with the monotonous straightness of its construction ; but nothing can exceed the vexatious nature of these twisting Cornish lanes which enlarge the distance from place to place amazingly. They are beautiful, it is true, very beautiful ; often overhung with trees whose topmost branches intertwine, and through which the sunlight pierces its way with difficulty, tracing strange Oriental patterns on the road ; some-times walled in with high banks covered with flowers, or loose-jointed stone walls in whose interstices ferns and sedums flourish ; but nevertheless they are better designed for an inconsequent stroll than for the speedy attainment of any definite goal. It was by way of these twisting lanes that Stephen and Elfride were supposed to have reached *Endelstow House*—the seat of Lord Luxellian. Whether such a house ever existed in the locality is doubtful : certainly there is no such place at the present time ; though

133.—St. Juliot Church from Vallency Valley.

134.—Pentargan Bay.

there is one answering to the description some twenty miles south of this parish. Anyhow, its position in the story may be gauged as being somewhere between *East* and *West Endelstow* villages.

The next scene we shall inquire into is one in which the cliffs formed the background. Stephen and Elfride had a memorable expedition to "the cliffs beyond Targan Bay." The direction they took, combined with the fact that the cliff is later described as being the second highest in the vicinity, leads us to infer that the reference is to the precipitous verge known locally as "Strangles," a name the origin of which is not clear. Nearly the whole of the coastline of this district is wild in the extreme ; jagged black rocks rise sheerly from the sea, forming precipitous walls, cruel and forbidding in appearance, and dangerous to walk upon. By inquiring our way to Strangles Cliff we shall in due course light upon a scene which seems vividly familiar to those of us who have read "A Pair of Blue Eyes." Beneath us is "the everlasting stretch of ocean." There are the "detached rocks," the "white screaming gulls," the "toothed and zig-zag line of storm-torn heights." With a westerly or north-westerly wind urging them onwards, the waves hurl themselves against the craggy cliff-face with terrific force, and a noise as of thunder which is deafening to listen to ; the wind seems to clutch at the clumps of heather and gorse and rough grass as though the tentacles of some giant octopus were grasping to wrench them from the soil. The seabirds wheel and dart and scream ; and far overhead may be seen the lordly peregrine falcon—now becoming so rare in our islands—sailing on outstretched pinions, or darting forward with his marvellously rapid flight, or stooping to some quarry on the earth far below him. The scene is bright and gay when the sun is shining, but when the sky is overcast with clouds a subtle sullenness seems to settle down on sea and land, and hang like an oppressive weight over all nature.

Later on in the story we visit the same spot with
Elfride and Knight, and on that occasion our author
gives this cliff the name of *Windy Beak*—a title which
was probably suggested to him by Cam Beak, a cliff
jutting out into the sea farther to the north.

Another sea-picture comes before our eyes when
we read of Knight and Elfride visiting *Targan Bay* on
their way to the scene of the adventure which so nearly
proved disastrous. There can be very little doubt in
our minds that *Targan Bay* was drawn from Pentargan,
a narrow inlet scarcely deserving the name of bay,
which lies a short two miles from Boscastle northwards (134). The description given us of the journey
thither from *Endelstow* vicarage is a true facsimile
of what we see to-day. There are still the "neutral
green hills," the "chocolate-toned rocks" on both sides
of the steep roads. We will follow in the footsteps
of Elfride when, starting from the vicarage, she
"ascended and passed over a hill" until she came
to "a small stream. . . . It was smaller than that in
her own valley. . . . Bushes lined the slopes of its
shallow trough; but at the bottom, where the water
ran, was a soft green carpet, in a strip two or three
yards wide." We may take precisely the same track
and follow the stream until we reach the ledge of rock
over which it precipitates itself on to the rocks deep
below. It was at this spot that they paused—Knight
having now joined her—and gazed out to sea, noting
the "nebulous haze, stretching like gauze" over it.
This haze is one of the predominant characteristics of
the western coasts; for we note the same peculiarity
on the west coast of Wales and of Ireland.

If we visit this spot on a day when Nature is
morose in mood, the "nebulous haze" will appear as
a heavy, inky pall brooding over everything. The
cliffs and rocks are of a dingy slate-colour; slate-
coloured is the sea and the sky and the pebbles on the
strand; even the grass looks less green than murky.

Leaving the bay with its miniature beach, and the

flanking walls tunnelled with caves, we will turn our attention to the steep cliff farther on, which is known to readers as "the cliff without a name" (a statement afterwards qualified and explained in the preface to the later editions). To the local resident this cliff passes by the name of Beeny, or Beeny High Cliff. Granting our surmise as to the identity of *Targan Bay* to have been correct, then this unchristened cliff falls into position as Beeny in disguise. It is a dangerous spot, as are most of the cliffs on this wild, windwrecked coast, and has been the scene of more than one tragedy. Its colour of slate-black, or more strictly dark purple, adds to its forbidding appearance, only a few thin streaks of white marble breaking in a slight degree its sombre face (135). This cliff and one a little beyond share the local reputation of being the highest in Cornwall, controversy on the subject of its actual, measurable height often leading to staunch declarations and spirited retorts. "Haggard cliffs," says our author, "of every ugly altitude, are as common as sea-fowl along the line of coast between Exmoor and Land's End; but this out-flanked and encompassed specimen was the ugliest of them all"— a contention which few who know the coast will be prepared to deny.

Of *Castle Boterel* we hear several times in the course of the narrative. Its identity with Boscastle may be readily guessed at, although of course it was the Boscastle of forty or more years ago which our author looked on as his model (136). To-day it is a very favourite resort with tourists, who become familiar with its likeness in many of the carriages on the South-Western Railway. Once there was a Norman mansion standing here, and it was known as Bottreaux Castle (though an old resident gives it as Boterel), but only its site is visible as a grass-covered mound a short distance from the village up the Jordan Valley. The harbour is cunningly contrived: Nature has sheltered it to some extent by the prominent headland

135.—BEENY HIGH CLIFF (IN THE DISTANCE).

136.—BOSCASTLE HARBOUR.

called Penally Point; and human ingenuity has fashioned rough stone piers to complete the work. It is a tortuous passage, and ships have to be warped up to the landing-stage. Through the headland just referred to there is a blow-hole, and at a certain level of the tide the water spurts through this tunnel in a dense spray or jet, as though forced by some mechanical agency. Curious, eerie noises proceed from the opening. Just off Penally Point is a tiny rock-island, called Meachard Island, once doubtless joined to the mainland, a favourite breeding-place of many gulls. There is a curious tradition connected with the parish church of St. Symphorian, Forrabury, which stands high on Willapark Point, in full view of the Atlantic. The tower is without bells, and a ballad by the Cornish poet, Robert Stephen Hawker, tells of a ship bearing bells hither being wrecked outside the harbour, and that the sunk bells may be heard tolling beneath the waves.

The port and town itself has lost some of its former picturesqueness by the demolition of many of the older cottages and the erection of new villas of prosaic architectural form. The roofs are all of slate—in strong contrast to the thatch we generally find in the central and northern portions of Wessex—but that is only to be expected, since the famous slate quarries of Delabole are so close at hand. Luckily, however, much of this slate is of a pale grey colour, and it "weathers" to a shade by no means disagreeable to the eyes.

There are several backgrounds in this book which we cannot discover. These we shall therefore regard as being either entirely fictitious, imported from elsewhere, or as having disappeared during the time which has elapsed since the book was written. *Endelstow House* aforesaid, its lodge, the cottage inhabited by Stephen's father, and other features are among these. The "ancient manor - house" which is supposed to have stood close to the vicarage was very probably

drawn from an old house called Tregrylls, now entirely
demolished, but which used to stand on the other side
of the Vallency Valley.

With Plymouth (figuring under its own name) we
have little to do. We read of Stephen spending an
hour there whilst waiting for his train to London, and
walking on the Hoe, whence can be seen "the wide
Sound, the breakwater, the lighthouse on far-off
Eddystone." Thither, too, we may follow Elfride a
fortnight later, when she goes to join him there and
be married secretly. We may picture her leaving the
valley of her home and mounting to an open table-
land from whence she had a view of the sea. Once
again our interest is directed to Plymouth, on the
occasion of the supposed journey from London by
steamer. We see the travellers as they pass in
succession the Nore, the South Foreland, Dover,
Beachy Head, Southampton, Portland Bill, the Race,
the Chesil Beach, West Bay, Start Point, Bolt Head,
Forward Point, Berry Head, Prawle — till finally
Plymouth is reached.

St. Launce's is a town often receiving mention.
At the time the story opens it was the nearest railway
station to *Endelstow* (137). To it rode Elfride on her
way to Plymouth, mentioned just above. "Presently the
quaint gables and jumbled roofs of St. Launce's were
spread beneath her, and going down the hill she entered
the courtyard of the Falcon." Launceston is surpris-
ingly full of interest to the archæologist and the antiquarian. Of its history prior to the Conquest little is
known, but the finding of Roman coins in the vicinity is
not without suggestion, and we may infer it possessed
a history anterior to that of the Norman invasion. At
one time the town was walled, and could show three
gateways, only one of which remains standing to-day.
The rooms above this archway are used as a museum
and contain many exceedingly interesting antiquities.
Probably the "White Hart Hotel" served our author
as original for the *Falcon* (138). It has a fine Norman

doorway, once pertaining to the Abbey which stood close to St. Thomas's Church, but of which nothing remains save the ruins. No one can visit Launceston without being struck by the ornate character of the parish church of St. Mary Magdalene, an early Tudor erection. The elaborate carving on the outer walls is teeming with interesting designs, but unfortunately its aspect is much marred by an incongruous figure in pink terra-cotta which stands in a niche over the south porch. The tower, which is at least a century older than the church, was originally detached from it, but is now joined by a building used as a vestry, but once a shop.

The most noteworthy feature of the town is undoubtedly the Castle, which stands on an eminence, its circular keep overtopping the town beneath. From the apex of the keep extends a marvellous view on all sides, proving the importance which must have at one time attached to the ancient fortress.

For a little while the action is diverted to London, whither it is needless for us to track the characters. *Bede's Inn* (probably Clement's Inn), Kensington, Hyde Park, the Drive and the Row, require no time to be spent in describing them. Killarney, as well as the foreign towns mentioned, we shall leave discreetly alone.

The house in which Mrs. Swancourt was supposed to reside was called *The Crags*, but we can find no trace of it to-day. Mention is made of a rock in the valley which had the contour of a man's face. There are many craggy rocks in the Vallency Valley, but we fail to recognise this particular one, though such contours do occur hereabout, and mature acquaintance with our author's methods leads us to assume that such a rock did actually exist there at the time the book was written; but weather-action will soon alter such characteristics or entirely efface them in a comparatively short time. Mrs. Jethway's cottage stands by the brook in the Vallency Valley, about half-way

137.—LAUNCESTON.

138.—THE WHITE HART HOTEL, LAUNCESTON.

between *Endelstow Vicarage* and *Castle Boterel*, and
has been repaired and brightened up since the time
of the story.

Of all the churches in the vicinity perhaps that of
Lesnewth may be taken as most nearly approximating
to the one called *East Endelstow*: we have already
seen its pinnacled tower from the valley road (139).

Our survey is now almost ended. The penultimate

139.—LESNEWTH CHURCH.

background is at *Camelton* railway station—distinctly suggestive of Camelford. Here we read of
Knight and Stephen arriving one night in company
with the "sombre van" which had travelled down on
the same train as themselves. We may track them
walking "in the darkness up the miles of road from
Camelton to Endelstow." They paused for shelter
from the rain at the blacksmith's shop—a place which
is found by inquiry from local inhabitants to have
been closed "this many years." It was here they first
learnt of Elfride's marriage to Lord Luxellian and

were shown the coffin-plate. Subsequently they entered an inn called the *Welcome Home* to obtain further particulars. Of this inn we can discover no sure trace; it partially recalls "The Ship" at Boscastle.

We may imagine them when on the following day they walk "up the familiar valley (Vallency Valley) to East Endelstow church" to attend the funeral. And after it is over we picture them retracing their steps "down the grey still valley to Castle Boterel."

CHAPTER II

"THE TRUMPET-MAJOR AND ROBERT HIS BROTHER"

THE plot of this romance rests on the anticipated landing of Napoleon in England, and is based—we are told in the preface—on facts that were handed down to posterity by local individuals who were themselves actively interested. The shadow cast by Napoleon on the southern coast of Wessex was of sufficient density to make the fact of his landing appear strangely probable. If to the actual evidence of his intended visit we add the influence of naturally superstitious temperaments, we need not be surprised to hear of the consequent precautions taken by the inhabitants of the towns and villages near the coast to guard against being caught unawares; of the systematic training of the local men; or the storage of weapons and ammunition in churches and similar safe retreats. Nor can we doubt that the elaborate arrangements made by many of the better-class people, to fly inland directly the news of his accomplished landing was flashed abroad by the beacon fires prepared on the hills, were the result of actual fear.

The country which forms the groundwork for the chief scenes lies in and around *Budmouth*—a place which we shall regard as being typical of Weymouth. If we accept *Overcombe* as representing Sutton Poyntz, a village lying just under Bincombe Down, it must not be in too narrow a sense, restricted by the actual confines of that village, since it embraces certain features of Upwey, and perhaps Bincombe too (140).

184

140.—BINCOMBE CHURCH.

141.—UPWEY MILL.

THE WESSEX OF THOMAS HARDY

The action commences here, at *Overcombe*—that is to say, as far as the local situation is concerned. The mill is drawn, not from the mill which once stood in the village of Sutton Poyntz, but from the one it probably resembled—that at Upwey, which we may see still exhibiting many of the features described in the book (141). Let us, then, imagine the Upwey mill to be standing in the village of Sutton Poyntz, where we also find the "large, smooth mill-pond" of our author's imagining, in which the cavalry watered their horses, and which was in full view of Ann Garland's window (142).

"On the other side of the mill-pond was an open cross," we read; it is quickly revealed to us as we stand beside the mill-pond. "Behind this a steep slope rose high into the sky, merging in a wide and open down." This description we likewise easily verify. We shall examine the down again when the scenery of "The Dynasts" comes before us. It is one of those features occurring in the Wessex Novels and Poems which remains precisely the same, year in and year out; it has been very little tampered with, and looks the same to-day as it did when the White Horse was being cut out by the encamping soldiery and the sweeping undulations were dotted with gorgeous uniforms and white canvas.

Our interest is quickly aroused in this down, and in fancy we watch the pitching of the tents and the various other arrangements consequent on the arrival of the soldiers, including the work of "making a zig-zag path down the incline from the camp to the river-head." This track may still be discerned and followed. When the novel appeared an old gentleman of ninety wrote to inform the author that he witnessed the arrival, which was exactly as described.

We may make up our minds to recognise Poxwell Hall as the prototype of the *Oxwell Hall* of the story, the home of Squire Derriman. Its "grey, weather-worn front" is familiar to every traveller passing it on the Weymouth-Wareham road (143). The fine old

142.—SUTTON POYNTZ.

143.—POXWELL HOUSE.

gate-house lends it an intensified interest, although this has been altered considerably from what it was pictured in the story.

Warmwell seems by its position to suggest *Springham* — the village whither Ann journeyed to the christening party.

Budmouth itself often claims our attention. It was when the king was on his way thither that the *Overcombe* folk climbed to the top of the Ridgeway to see him pass. He was to change horses at " Woodyates Inn " — a hostel near Cranborne which still bears traces of its former importance as a posting-house. The miller and his party waited at the summit of the hill until after "the bell of St. Peter's, Casterbridge—in E flat "—a fine note, still to be heard—had chimed three o'clock, when the long-expected cortege at length came in sight on "the white line of road " (144). We can well imagine the enthusiasm which filled the hearts of the villagers as they shouted " Long life to King Jarge." These were stirring times, and excitement ran high when the routine of daily life was broken in upon by the sudden advent of the soldiers on the down. People frequently went to visit the encampment, and we see the miller taking his friends there on a Sunday evening.

When the review was held, " the whole population of Overcombe . . . ascended the slope with the crowds from afar," and if we follow them in imagination we may hear the exclamations which burst from the lips of the onlookers. It was while witnessing these excitements that Miller Loveday was apprised of the fact that a letter waited for him at the *Budmouth* post office; and it drew from him the remark that "there *was* a letter in the candle " (145). This interesting superstition has almost died out, disappearing concurrently with the " tallow dip," but it still persists here and there in " outstep placen." The letter heralds the coming of Bob Loveday, and soon after his arrival we read of him journeying to *Casterbridge* (Dorchester) to meet

144.—View from Ridgeway Hill, looking towards Dorchester.

145.—The Statue of King George, Weymouth.

189

his fiancée. The "Old Greyhound Inn," where he puts up his horse, is still to be found in South Street, but has long lost its licence. We see him standing at the Bow watching the road in the direction of Grey's Bridge, until he sees the coach from *Melchester*—the city we have come to look at as closely resembling Salisbury—where his lady-love had been staying with her aunt. But as she does not arrive, he beguiles the hours by "wandering up and down the pavement," evidently somewhere close to the church of All-Saints, since the voices of the worshippers come to him through the open windows.

The soldiers go into barracks at *Exonbury*—the city we think of as Exeter. We are recalled to the down by the kindling of the beacon fire, an incident repeated in "The Dynasts"; and as we shall examine this later on it need not detain us now. The alarm had the effect of sending the women-folk inland, and amongst the refugees we see our friends from *Overcombe Mill* hastening towards *Kingsbere*—the townlet we have already recognised as Bere Regis. The old order for their retreat thither still exists. They were pursued by Festus Derriman, after he had learned to his satisfaction and relief that the report of Napoleon's landing was false. He "cantered on over the hill (Ridgeway), meeting on his route the Lower Longpuddle or Weatherbury (Puddletown) volunteers." The lonely cottage in which he besieged Ann is still to be seen amid the farther downs above Holcombe Bottom, but it is now in a state of complete ruin.

The episode of the press-gang brings before us very vividly the date at which the incidents were imagined to have taken place, for impressment died out at the end of the Napoleonic wars in 1815. We see Ann driving back from *Budmouth* with her lover; she glances apprehensively in the direction of the ships lying at anchor in the bay towards Portland, whose "dark contour, lying like a whale on the sea," is readily discerned.

146.—THE WHITE HORSE, PRESTON.

147.—LOOKING UP THE HARBOUR, WEYMOUTH.

We may now follow the Trumpet-Major and Ann when they go to see the White Horse, cut out on the chalky hill-side by the soldiers (146). "After pacing from the horse's head down his breast to his hoof, back by way of the king's bridle-arm, past the bridge of his nose, and into his cocked hat, Ann said that she had had enough of it, and stepped out of the chalk clearing upon the grass. The Trumpet-Major had remained all the time in a melancholy attitude within the rowel of his Majesty's right spur." We may follow either of these actions. The easiest ascent to the White Horse is from Sutton Poyntz; but if we walk along the top of the ridge from Bincombe Down, and turn to the right over the crest of the hill, thus suddenly finding ourselves surrounded by patches of bare, chalky earth, we shall be set wondering as to their meaning, for no resemblance can be traced to the horse or its rider as they appear from the opposite hill, where the road winds up from Preston Village.

Pos'ham, which is the colloquial rendering of Portesham, was the birthplace of Captain Hardy— Nelson's Hardy—one of a collateral branch of the Dorset Hardys—and in the village we can find his house; while the steep hill going northwards out of the village will bring us to the monument which stands solitary on Blagdon, or Blackdown. In the story, Bob visits the Captain in his home, and the result of his interview is that he joins the *Victory* and sails away.

Portland Bill, or Beal, comes before us as a vantage-point when Ann goes there to catch a last glimpse of the ship. We may picture her journey by carrier to *Budmouth* (147); then, crossing the Fleet in a rowing-boat—for a bridge was lacking at that time,—she climbs the steep road to the top of Portland—"the huge lump of freestone which forms the peninsula"— and in due course reaches "the extreme southerly peak of rock" from which she watches "the great silent ship" as it passes and disappears. We shall visit "the wild, herbless, weather-worn promontory" again, when we

search for the scenery figuring in the poem entitled
" Souls of the Slain."

After Bob's departure on board the *Victory* we see
Ann and John walking side by side until they come to
" a gable, known as Faringdon Ruin," under which title
it still may be found in Came Park, close to Dorchester,

148.—FARINGDON RUIN.

and is all that now remains of the church and the village
which once stood there (148).

This meeting prepares us for the closing incidents
of the story. " Uncle Benjy " dies, and *Oxwell Hall*,
with its " muddy quadrangle, archways, mullioned
windows, cracked battlements, and weed-grown garden,"
becomes the property of Ann Garland. And from the
doors of the familiar mill we catch our last glimpse of
John as he " marches into the night."

CHAPTER III

"TWO ON A TOWER"

In the preface to this book we are told that "the scene of action was suggested by two real spots in the part of the country specified, each of which has a column standing upon it. Certain surrounding peculiarities have been imported into the narrative from both sides." The characteristics pertaining to the two spots are easily determined. The actual building is drawn in the main from the tower standing in Charborough Park, a few miles south of Wimborne Minster (149); while the immediate setting of the fictitious observatory shows us the position occupied by a shaft or obelisk which rises from a hill near Milborne St. Andrew, between Blandford and Dorchester.

We will examine the situation first. To quote from the book : " The central feature of the middle distance . . . was a circular isolated hill . . . covered with fir-trees. . . ." The obelisk is known locally as " Milborne Speer " or " Ring's-Hill Speer "—the latter title being an allusion to the entrenched earthwork from which the spire rises. Some few years ago the trees on the summit of the hill were thinned, and to-day the spire stands out boldly before the eyes of the traveller on the Dorchester-Blandford road. The monument bears the date of 1761 ; it is built chiefly of brick, with stone quoins ; the initials " E. M. P." stand for Edmund Morton Pleydell, in whose memory it was erected.

The origin of the earthwork is open to question—

149.—CHARBOROUGH PARK ENTRANCE GATES.

150.—CHARBOROUGH TOWER.

195

a fact to which our author draws attention. "The fir-shrouded hill-top was (according to some antiquaries) an old Roman camp,—if it were not (as others insisted) an old British castle, or (as the rest swore) an old Saxon field of Witenagemote,—with remains of an outer and inner vallum." If we visit the spot in spring we shall be struck at once with the natural wild-flower garden which surrounds the spire. Bluebells, cowslips, campions in many shades of red and pink, whitethorn, and the mealy guelder-rose literally cover the ground. As though to impress us with its isolated position, we may see hovering over the spot the kestrels which nest there almost every year, and have done from time immemorial. The original trenches are almost level with the banks, for the fir-needles have dropped into them year after year, and the footfalls of a visitor are muffled as though he trod a pile carpet. The earthwork is known as Weatherbury Castle, and hints to us whence came our author's fictitious name for Puddletown.

The tower in Charborough Park—more particularly the column of the novel—is 120 feet in height, and from the summit extends a magnificent view of the surrounding country. It is a conspicuous landmark, visible from a distance of many miles and from several different directions. It is described in the book as having been built "in the Tuscan order of classic architecture," which is literally correct (150).

A flight of wide, moss-grown steps leads up to the tower; the exterior is decorated with some interesting grotesques. Just inside is a tablet which tells us the tower was erected in 1790, was struck by lightning in 1838, and was considerably damaged. In the year following it was rebuilt, forty feet being added. A heavy moulded handrail guides us to the top, where we enter a room panelled in chestnut and fitted with some handsomely carved seats, from whence the view is seen through the many windows. We recognise the Hardy Monument on Blackdown; the long range of the Purbeck Hills; Bournemouth, backed by the New Forest; Studland; and a portion of the Channel. With a pair of glasses we should make out many familiar landmarks.

Close to this tower is Charborough House, the prototype of the *Welland House* of the story (151). It stands in a finely timbered park, wherein is a magnificent herd of deer, also some cattle of Asiatic breed. In the grounds is an interesting grotto, the front surmounted by a figure of Fame, and bearing an inscription recording the fact that the plan of the Great Revolution was formulated therein in the year 1686. Near the house is the church; this and the adjacent graveyard form the backgrounds for some short scenes.

Wimborne Minster, in its fictitious presentment of *Warborne*, interests us as being the place where St. Cleeve was supposed to be educated. According to Haymoss, it was "a place where they draw up young gam'sters' brains like rhubarb under a ninepenny pan." The first college was founded here in 1043 by Edward the Confessor, and remained unaltered until 1496, when Margaret of Richmond founded a chantry and established a school in connection with it. The old Grammar School buildings were demolished and new ones erected in 1851 (152). Wimborne is an ancient town, thought by some to be identical with the Vindogladia of the Antonine Itinerary. The fine church or minster forms the most notable feature, the central part dating from the twelfth century; it contains many interesting monuments, including a brass bearing the date of 873, supposed to mark the resting-place of King Æthelred. Under the west tower is an orrery clock, which is said to have been going since the fourteenth century, and which was made by Peter Lightfoot, a monk of Glastonbury. In the chapel of Holy Trinity is a Saxon chest 1100 years old. In a room above the vestry is the famous chained library, founded in the sixteenth century.

151.—CHARBOROUGH HOUSE.

152.—THE MINSTER AND GRAMMAR SCHOOL, WIMBORNE.

153.—WINTERBORNE ZELSTONE.

154.—THE PALACE, SALISBURY.

THE WESSEX OF THOMAS HARDY

Little Welland Village would seem to be more or less a counterpart of Winterborne Zelstone (153); its importance in the action of the narrative is not great. The "venerable thatched house . . . built of chalk in the lump," in which St. Cleeve was imagined to have lived, cannot now be found, and has probably perished since the time of the story.

The city of Bath figures under its own name and forms one of the backgrounds. Here we can picture Lady Constantine "wandering about beneath the aisles" of the Abbey. Bath, that place of steep, abrupt hills, terraced to accommodate the roads and houses rising in tiers above the valley of the Avon, with its two distinct legends ascribing the foundation of the city to a British king, Bladud, is too well known to need description. The mineral springs from which it takes its name were long used by the Romans, and the Baths are justly considered to represent one of the finest Roman antiquities in Western Europe.

Greenwich Observatory, Southampton Docks, and The Cape figure in this novel to some extent; then for a time the action takes us to *Melchester*, which is tantamount to Salisbury. Here we read of the "precincts of the damp and venerable Close," and are presently introduced to the "episcopal palace," depicted doubtless from the picturesque irregular building which is still the residence of the bishop (154).

CHAPTER IV

"THE WELL-BELOVED"

(*A Sketch of a Temperament*)

IT is to Portland, "the Peninsula carved by Time out of a single stone," that we must go to find the surroundings which served for this romance—or satire. Nearly all the action takes place here, on this mysterious storm-lashed eminence, known to us in the Wessex Novels and Poems as "The Isle of Slingers," "The Isle by the Race," and other titles similarly descriptive of Portland. Commonly designated an island, it is in reality a peninsula, connected with the mainland by a thin neck of pebbles called the Chesil Beach, or Bank —chesil being derived from an Anglo-Saxon word meaning pebble. The Bank varies in width, but is at no point wider than two hundred yards. The gales which sweep over it from the south-west are phenomenal in force, coming straight off the Atlantic, and the waves in the West Bay, or Deadman's Bay, are literally mountains high. The present writer has driven along the road in a dog-cart more than once when the vehicle has been swung half round by the force of the wind. Deadman's Bay is well named, for if a vessel once gets inside it during a gale, there is only the remotest possibility of its ever getting out again, and a practical certainty of its being dashed to pieces on the beach.

The Island—to call it by its colloquial name—has

an atmosphere splendidly curative of chest diseases, as shown by its effect on soldiers quartered there. The cliffs are precipitous, and only a few spots on the southern side are accessible from the sea. Although subdivided into several villages, to the Islanders themselves there seem to be two main distinctive divisions— " Top o' Hill " and " Under Hill." Its ancient history is difficult to discover with any great exactness. Saxon, Roman, and Dane all had their day without doubt, but very few records remain to testify to the length of their occupation. The old-time barrows, the earthworks, the stone circles, all of which were represented half a century ago, have been destroyed by quarry extensions and building operations. Portland is connected in most people's minds with the convict establishment—that fastness from which it is boasted no prisoner has escaped alive ; in fact, every visitor who goes to the Island to-day is accosted by numerous would-be guides, eager to take him to spots from which the convicts may be seen at work. For those who are of a sufficiently morbid turn of mind it is possible, or used to be quite recently, to obtain for the modest sum of sixpence a tea which includes a window-sight of the prison yard! The majority of us will probably be satisfied with a ramble over the Island and a look at some of the quarries which have become world-famous. The oölitic limestone obtained here has been used for many important buildings in the country, including St. Paul's Cathedral.

We are told in the preface that this is the " home of a curious and well-nigh distinct people, cherishing strange beliefs and singular customs now for the most part obsolescent." It is with regret that we notice the extermination of these idiosyncrasies, for Portland has altered out of all recognition during the last few generations. Naturally, any sort of insulation tends to keep back progress of the race, particularly as regards mental development, and until recent years the Islanders were a long way behind the dwellers on the mainland in point of intellectual advancement; and whilst we may, from one standpoint, decry this backwardness, we cannot but appreciate a fact which enabled us to retrace a page in the history of human evolution and gaze on a past link in the chain of life. Similarly, we view the immutable rock which, formed countless centuries ago, has resisted Time's onslaughts till now, and gives itself up grudgingly to the scientifically designed tools and engines in the hands of the quarriers.

With an upward intellectual trend has also occurred a deterioration of physique, accompanied by a more lax moral standard. A point of strange interest to the anthropologist was the fact that, although intermarriage between near relatives was common, yet the mental and physical characteristics of the people displayed no ill effects therefrom. The custom of close-marriage in the Island was due partly to necessity—owing to the isolation and difficulty of communion with neighbouring people—and partly to an unwritten code whereby the people sought to keep themselves distinct. Even nowadays the names are limited in number—a feature which comes before us in the case of many islands and districts naturally isolated. The innate pride of the Portlander still makes him keenly conscious of the distinction between those born on the Island and the stranger, or "kimberlin." The present writer was at Portland recently and entered into conversation with a local man, intimating at the outset that he was merely a kimberlin; to which the Islander replied, "Oh well, I'm a thoroughbred 'un." It was said, too, with an air of conscious superiority which was not lost on his listener. Patriotism is another marked characteristic on this rocky island home. It was one day at the Beal that a casual chat with another of the Islanders brought out his love of the homeland. He had been a soldier, had served in the South African and other campaigns, had visited many of the beauty spots of the world; but nowhere had he found any scenery that appealed to him as did the wild storm-lashed rocks of Portland, where he hoped to live out the rest of his life and be gathered to his fathers in the wind-swept churchyard.

Portland always seems as though wrapped in a cloak of sadness, and holds a sombre atmosphere of which it grows impossible to be oblivious. The countless æons of time through which our world has been built up is very manifest here, for the geological epochs are strongly marked—a fact sufficient in itself to produce a sobering influence on our minds.

We will now follow Pierston in imagination as he comes upon the scene. Through the *Street of Wells* (Fortune's Well) he passes, and, after a stiff climb up the precipitous hill, walks towards the *Eastern Village* —doubtless a designation of Easton. Here we see him pause before the cottage in which the Caros lived. Coming before the closed gates which form the northern entrance to Pennsylvania Castle (155), we note a lane on our left hand, and at the corner stands the model of the Caros' home. "Like the Island it was all of stone, not only in walls but in window frames, roof, chimneys, fence, stile, pigstye and stable, almost door." Many of these descriptive features may be traced to-day, though certain innovations have crept in which have not added to picturesqueness. It stood close to the house of Pierston's father, the two gardens adjoining (156).

Pierston renews his early acquaintance with Avice, and soon we watch them taking walks about the Island, visiting the Bill or Beal, and "pausing over the treacherous cavern known as Cave Hole" (157). We are led to the Beal frequently in our explorations; we go thither with Ann Garland in "The Trumpet-Major," and again when it forms the background for the poem entitled "The Souls of the Slain." Cave Hole is one of the many caverns which abound on the Island; its actual position is difficult to describe, but may be easily found by inquiry of a local person. Then we may

155.—Entrance to Pennsylvania Castle, Portland.

156.—Cottage near Church-Hope, Portland.

205

picture Pierston descending the hill to listen to Avice singing at the village hall, and we may follow them on their subsequent return homewards together. We see them in our mind's eye climbing up the steep hill and pausing at the top to gaze over the bay before them, whence " there arose a deep, hollow stroke like the single beat of a drum, the intervals being filled with a long drawn rattling, as of bones between huge canine jaws. It came from the vast concave of Deadman's Bay, rising and falling against the pebble dyke." If we wish to appreciate this truly realistic description we must stand on the hill-top when night is falling or after darkness has set in. Then we may absorb to the full the strange weirdness of this rocky island and become as it were impregnated with the atmosphere which clings to it. Then, and then only, can we hope to obtain a true impression of that "sinister bay," or feel the existence of " the human multitude lying below; those who had gone down in vessels of war, East Indiamen, barges, brigs, and ships of the Armada— select people, common and debased. . . ."

The old graveyard of Church-Hope was supposed to be visited. Of the church itself we can see little to-day, but the headstones around it testify that long-perished inhabitants lie here at rest, in a position hard to beat from the point of view of picturesqueness (158). The whole mass seems to have slipped down the side of the cliff and narrowly escaped being precipitated into the sea below. This is the most interesting portion of the Island to the botanist; the cliffs here are clothed in wild-flowers, rocks jutting out between the patches of blossoms and forming a rock-garden of nature's fashioning which throws all artificial attempts at emulation into the shade. Just below, the sea washes gently on the sandy beach of the little cove; and as though guarding it from peril there stand the remains of the *Red King's Castle*—Rufus Castle, or Bow-and-Arrow Castle, as it is alternatively called—the very name testifying to the period at which it was built (159).

157.—CAVE HOLE, PORTLAND.

158.—CHURCH-HOPE, PORTLAND.

207

When Pennsylvania Castle, in the guise of *Sylvania Castle*, comes before us it is the residence of Marcia Bencomb for the time being. This castle is a comparatively modern building, erected by John Penn, grandson of William Penn, once a governor of Portland and the founder of Pennsylvania (160). To use our author's words : " It is a private mansion of comparatively modern date, in whose grounds stood the single plantation of trees of which the Island could boast. . . ."

We will follow in Pierston's footsteps when he sets out to walk to *Budmouth-Regis*—approximately Weymouth—by way of the Chesil Beach. It was when a gale was blowing and the rain had "assumed the character of a raking fusillade." We see him overtaking Marcia, and we watch them seeking shelter under one of the upturned lerrets. After a time they renew the struggle to reach *Budmouth*, cross the ferry-bridge—now represented by a more permanent structure—leave the ruined castle of Sandsfoot on their right hand, and finally enter the town, where they sleep the night at a temperance inn near the station. The next morning they journey to London by train ; thither we shall not follow them.

An interval of nearly twenty years elapses before we visit Portland again—this time by train—passing close under Sandsfoot Castle, the fort erected by Henry VIII. for the protection of the shipping (161). A familiar scene comes before our eyes as we catch sight of the "black lerrets" and "the white cubes of oolite"; and then we climb the accustomed hill and pass across the plateau to the ruined Church-Hope, stranded half-way down the cliff-face. Here, at the graveside of Avice, Pierston sees her daughter. Shortly after this encounter, we read of him as the tenant of *Sylvania Castle*, and we picture him on the evening of his arrival inspecting the house, the garden, and then entering the "garden-house of Elizabethan design, which stood on the outer walls of the grounds, and commanded by a

159.—Rufus Castle, Portland.

160.—Pennsylvania Castle, Portland.

window . . . the home of the resuscitated Avice." We may follow him on a subsequent evening when he is imagined walking down the lane to the *Red King's Castle* and searching for the names of Avice and Jocelyn, cut by himself years ago on one of the blocks of stone which had once formed a portion of the castle, but which now lay on the cliff-side below.

A further interval of time, during which our principal characters are in London and elsewhere, and we again visit Portland. Pierston is imagined to be staying for a time at *Budmouth*, and he frequently journeys to the Island. It is now that he becomes acquainted with the third Avice. *Henry the Eighth's Castle*, which we look on as the fictitious presentment of Sandsfoot Castle, comes before us again as the stage of events. Here, "on the verge of the ragstone cliff," Pierston meets Avice—at the same spot where he had arranged to meet the first Avice forty years previously. Hope Cove, the beautiful little bay which we have already regarded from Church-Hope, marks the spot from whence Avice and Leverre are supposed to have escaped in a rowing boat that had neither oars nor sails (162). It will be remembered that they came perilously near being drowned, for they had drifted very close to the Race, that dangerous current which even large vessels avoid in rough weather, and which is dangerous to small boats at any time. Its churned waters and white-capped waves may be seen most readily from the Beal, looking towards the Shambles, a sandbank lying towards the south-east.

It is at Portland that we first become acquainted with Pierston, and here likewise we catch our last glimpse of him, living in a house at "the top of the Street of Wells"—a house we cannot identify with any certainty—and strolling with Marcia "towards the Beal, or the ancient Castle."

161.—Sandsfoot Castle.

162.—Hope Cove, Portland.

CHAPTER V

DAME THE FIRST

The First Countess of Wessex

THE first description which we have to examine is *King's Hintock Court*—"one of the most imposing of the mansions that overlook our beautiful Blackmoor or Blakemoor Vale." This was probably drawn from Melbury House, near Evershot, a mansion partly of Elizabethan design, standing in a park containing several lakes and some fine timber, including a magnificent double avenue of sycamores.

In *Falls-Park* we recognise a likeness to Mells, the description of the mansion and its environs enabling us to identify it with some degree of certainty. "Its classic front, of the period of the second Charles . . . the densely-timbered Park . . ." strikes the beholder with a certain sense of familiarity when he sees Mells before him. The theatre of the story is continually changing as we follow the fortunes of "Mistress Betty." We picture Squire Dornell leaving Mells, and riding "along the dead level which stretches between the hills skirting Falls-Park and those bounding the town of Ivell (assumed to be Yeovil)," as he makes his way to *King's Hintock Court*. Certain friends come to him here, amongst them "the doctor from Evershead (Evershot) . . . Baxby of Sherton Castle (Sherborne)." *Evershead* is the village to

212

163.—The Acorn Inn, Evershot.

164.—Horton Inn.

which Tupcombe rides to learn news of Betty, and we see him in imagination halting at the *Sow-and-Acorn*— obviously sketched from the present "Acorn Inn" (163).

Of the position of the house fictitiously called *Elm-Cranlynch* we have no clue, though we may not be altogether wide of the mark in finding a connection between it and Montacute, an Elizabethan mansion standing in a picturesque village four miles west of Yeovil, near the "view tower" which occupies the site of one of William the Conqueror's strongholds.

We read of the Squire's ride to Bristol, and of Betty's subsequent elopement. We will follow her when, in company with Phelipson, she leaves the Court "by an obscure gate to the east," and in due time enters "the solitary length of the old Roman road now called Long Ash Lane"—a road we have explored in the short story entitled "Interlopers at the Knap." It may be mentioned in passing that the wretchedly deficient nomenclature of the new ordnance maps is shown by the fact that, though this lane is named in the old copies, the recently issued ones leave it undesignated. They are supposed to have halted at a "mean roadside inn." Stagg's Folly, Prince's Place, or Southfield Hill—lonely houses on that highway—more or less demolished since the date of the story—might have indicated the locality of the inn.

Dame the Second

Barbara of the House of Grebe

This grim tale opens at a point on the "turnpike-road connecting Havenpool (Poole) and Warborne (Wimborne) with the city of Melchester (Salisbury)." In *Knollingwood Hall* we trace a resemblance to the mansion in St. Giles Park, about two miles south of Cranborne. This fine example of battlemented architecture dates from the sixteenth century and encloses a quadrangular court ; but much of the original building has been renovated or rebuilt. It is famous as the birthplace of Anthony Cooper, afterwards Baron Ashley. In the grounds is a grotto, constructed principally of Indian shells, which is said to have cost £10,000. It is stated that the first cabbage grown in England was cultivated in the garden of St. Giles.

Chene Manor is more or less portrayed from Canford Manor, and was the supposititious residence of Sir John and Lady Grebe. The mansion was rebuilt during the last century, but some of the older portions remain, including "John of Gaunt's Kitchen," with its huge fireplace and many ancient cooking vessels.

Lornton Inn is described as "the rendezvous of many a daring poacher for operations in the adjoining forest." Horton Inn, which is its prototype, stands at the cross-roads about four miles from Wimborne, and was at one time a noted posting-house where the stage-coaches proceeding from London to Exeter were accustomed to change horses (164).

The *Yewsholt Lodge* of the story—"a small place on the plan of a large one"—was the house pictured as the scene of Barbara's ghastly experience after her marriage, and if we would find the model that served our author we must go to the little hamlet of Farrs, about a mile and a half to the west of Wimborne, where such a secluded house, with a small gallery round the hall, is still standing.

Dame the Third

The Marchioness of Stonehenge

There is very little in this story for the topographer to unravel. The Marchioness "lived in a classical mansion . . . not a hundred miles from the city of Melchester" (we read), and we recognise it as a fictitious presentment of Wilton House, near Salisbury (165-167). This historic mansion teems with interest. According to tradition, Shakespeare is supposed to

165.—WILTON HOUSE.

166.—THE BRIDGE, WILTON HOUSE.

167.—The Terrace, Wilton House.

168.—Winchester Cathedral.

THE WESSEX OF THOMAS HARDY

have played here with his company before James I. ;
the picture galleries, containing a superb collection of
old masters, and including some fine examples of
Holbein, Vandyke, etc., are too well known to need
mention ; many marble statues adorn the entrance
hall and cloisters. The older portion of the house
is Italian sixteenth-century work. Wilton was a seat
of the West Saxon kings, and was at one time a town
of considerable prosperity.

Dame the Fourth

Lady Mottisfont

The first scene to which we are spirited in this
romance is the interior of Winchester Cathedral,
familiar to Hardy readers as *Wintoncester*, one of the
most fascinating of all the towns which figure in the
Wessex Novels, its charm being enhanced by its
situation in a deep hollow surrounded by chalky
downlands (168). The town has already come before
us in our explorations into the country of " Tess of the
d'Urbervilles," but our interest at the present juncture
is confined to the Cathedral.

It holds the record of being the longest cathedral
in England—about 556 feet from end to end. The
exterior suffers much as a whole from lacking all but
the base of the central tower, which is unobtrusive
and scarcely to be marked from any great distance.
Our author's description is so realistic that a vivid
impression remains in the reader's mind of the spot
whereon Sir Ashley Mottisfont is supposed to ask
Philippa to marry him.

We have nothing further to do with the town in
the story, but a ramble through Winton—to give it
its ancient name—must prove interesting. According
to tradition, it was first founded ninety-nine years
before the building of Rome. Research has revealed
that the Itchen Valley was once the home of Celtic

169.—BROADLANDS.

170.—EMBLEY HOUSE.

peoples ; and the fact that six Roman roads diverge from here goes to show its importance in Romano-British times. Its historical greatness commences perhaps at the date when it was the capital of Wessex; and when the kings of Wessex became the kings of England Winton was as much the capital of the country as London. Winton, too, must be ever associated in the mind with King Arthur and his knights.

Deansleigh Park, the home of Sir Ashley Mottis-font, may be sought for near Romsey, and we can safely regard Broadlands as the pattern present in our author's mind. This house stands just outside the town and can be seen from the bridge which we cross on entering the town from Salisbury (169). In *Fernell Hall* we find a resemblance to Embley House, famous from its association with Florence Nightingale (170). It stands about two miles west of Romsey on the Salisbury road. For a time the action turns to Bath, but it soon reverts to *Deansleigh Park* and the country around that spot.

DAME THE FIFTH

The Lady Icenway

"In 'a faire maner-place' . . . in one o' the greenest bits of woodland between Bristol and the city of Exonbury (Exeter)," lived Maria Heymere and her uncle. We find its counterpart in Longleat House, a magnificent mansion standing in its ancient deer park amid surrounding woods and forests which would be hard to equal in their display of timber and picturesque scenery (171). The house is distant five miles from the market-town of Warminster, which separated Salisbury Plain from the woods and meadow-lands. Warminster is mentioned in Domesday Book as a royal manor whose tenant was bound to provide a night's lodging for the king and his retinue—a mandate

171.—LONGLEAT.

172.—MARWELL HALL.

which was enforced by George III. when he visited Longleat. Longleat House is one of the largest, as also one of the most beautiful, in the county of Wilts, and dates from the sixteenth century. The word "leat" means a conduit, and refers in the present instance to the long narrow mere which crosses the park from north to south; formerly it conveyed water to the mill once attached to the priory which was founded at Horningham in the thirteenth century. The house was built by Sir John Thynne, but the name of its designer appears to be unknown. Its style is distinctly Italian; Doric, Ionic, and Corinthian orders being represented.

The only other place we have mention of is the house in which Maria is supposed to have lived after her marriage to Lord Icenway, and where Anderling followed her and subsequently died. For this we must travel "beyond Wintoncester, quite at t'other end of Wessex," until we reach Marwell Hall, famous as holding the coffer historically associated with "The Mistletoe Bough" (172).

Dame the Sixth

Squire Petrick's Lady

We are told at the outset that the "splendid old mansion" in *Stapleford* is now pulled down. *Stapleford* is typical of Stalbridge, and as in the tale nothing now remains of the real Stalbridge House; the park wall, and the gateway which opens into it, the gateposts adorned with a lion's head and trunk, are all that survive as indication of its former grandeur (173). The little town shows us a remarkably fine example of a market-cross; it is covered with elaborate carvings, is thirty feet in height, and dates probably from some time in the fourteenth century (174). The destruction of the house prevents our following the events within it (175).

173.—THE GATEWAY, STALBRIDGE PARK.

174.—THE MARKET-CROSS, STALBRIDGE.

175.—STALBRIDGE VILLAGE.

176.—SHERBORNE CASTLE.

"A GROUP OF NOBLE DAMES"

Dame the Seventh
Anna, Lady Baxby

This romance carries us a long way back in history, to the time of the Great Rebellion, when so many castles now in ruins were at the height of their prosperity. *Sherton Castle*, where almost the entire action takes place, is an instance in point, since only a few walls, mantled in ivy and overrun with vagrant greenery, remain to us to-day as evidence of the majestic building which once stood there (176-177). Sherborne, fictitiously presented as *Sherton Abbas*, has no indications of either Roman or British settlement, and its history probably dates only from after the Saxon conquest in the seventh century. Here, in the year 705, St. Aldhelm fixed his bishop's stool for the new diocese of Western Wessex. Ethelbert, king of Wessex, was buried here in 866 ; and for a time the town figured as the actual capital of Wessex.

The castle was built by Bishop Roger of Caen, and was once described by Henry of Huntingdon as being scarcely inferior to that of Devizes, "than which there was none greater within the confines of England." It passed through many vicissitudes. Owing to its strength, Stephen wrested it by force from Bishop Roger ; and later Elizabeth gave it to Sir Walter Raleigh, though only on a leasehold tenure.

In 1905 a pageant was invented and arranged in commemoration of the twelve hundredth anniversary of the town, the bishopric, and the school. This was held in the grounds of the old castle, and set the fashion for the successive pageants which have since taken place in other towns.

The story before us is based on historical facts, and we are told that " the Parliament forces sat down before Sherton Castle with over seven thousand foot and four pieces of cannon." The besiegers were under the command of Lady Baxby's brother—an obvious

225   Q

177.—SHERBORNE CASTLE.

178.—WOLFETON HOUSE.

pseudonym for Digby—and out of consideration for her he postponed hostilities for a time; but while he still hesitated to commence an attack Lord Baxby arrived with reinforcements, before whom he retreated "to a hill near Ivell (Yeovil), four or five miles off." For all this there is much foundation in local chronicles.

Sherborne possesses many objects of interest to the archæologist and the antiquarian. From 998 to 1539 it was the seat of a Benedictine Monastery, in which latter year its Abbey was dissolved. It was never a town protected by an enclosing wall, but depended on the fortified bishop's palace and its natural marshy environs for safety from invasion. King Alfred is supposed to have passed the greater portion of his boyhood here, and also to have received his education in this town. The handsome conduit standing in the old market-place—a spot depicted in "The Woodlanders"—dates from the sixteenth century; its building is attributed to Abbot Mere; it stood originally inside the Cloister Court of the Abbey Church, but was later moved to its present position.

The Abbey Church exhibits some Norman work; also a portion of outside wall generally attributed to a pre-Norman period; Early English and Perpendicular styles are also represented. Sherborne School and the Almshouse well repay careful inspection, though neither occur as features in the Wessex Novels.

Dame the Eighth

The Lady Penelope

The position of the house from which our author drew the first setting for this story is accurately described at the commencement of the narrative. "In going out of Casterbridge (Dorchester) by the low-lying road which eventually conducts to the town of Ivell (Yeovil), you see on the right hand an ivied manor-house, flanked by battlemented towers, and more than usually distinguished by the size of its many mullioned windows." The house is conspicuously prominent from the Great Western Railway line soon after the train emerges from Poundbury tunnel; it is called Wolfeton House and stands a little distance back from the high road (178); directly behind it is the village of Charminster, in the parish

179.—THE GATE-HOUSE, WOLFETON HOUSE.

church of which is the tomb marking the spot where the Lady Penelope and her last husband are supposed to have been buried. Whether this be so or not, her marriage with her three suitors successively is a fairly well known tradition.

Wolfeton House was rebuilt by one of the Trenchards during the reign of Henry VII., but certain portions exhibit unmistakable signs of having belonged to a period much earlier. The gate-house, with a round tower on each side, is probably of Norman origin (179). The interior of the house shows us some interesting and handsome carving.

A legend connects the dining-room with "the ghost of Lady Trenchard," which is supposed to have appeared previous to her death, the result of suicide.

PART III

NOVELS OF INGENUITY

CHAPTER I

THE first landscape of any importance in this novel is before us when we hear of the characters at *Budmouth*, a place already mentioned as being more or less typical of Weymouth ; and here we find the bay and the esplanade figuring as the principal backgrounds. If we follow Springrove and Owen and Cytherea Grey on the occasion when they take the excursion steamer to *Lulstead Cove*, we shall recognise a spot we have already visited when exploring the country of " Far from the Madding Crowd," this being the Cove where Troy bathed and was thought to have been drowned. We declared it then to symbolise Lulworth Cove. After they reach their destination we read that Owen goes off to visit " an interesting mediæval ruin," and we have little doubt that our author refers to Corfe Castle. Finding it is too late to catch the return boat he walks on to *Anglebury*—a place we shall refer to later. Returning to the Cove, we watch the passengers re-embarking " by the primitive plan of a narrow plank on two wheels "—a method which may still be seen there to-day. Lulworth was once the scene of considerable smuggling operations, the residents in the few thatched cottages combining fishing and smuggling as their means of livelihood ; but the little village is becoming rapidly crowded with week-end cottages and villas, which do not add to its picturesqueness or its charm.

233

Very soon after the *Lulstead* episode we see Springrove and Cytherea boating in *Budmouth Bay*, following the long line of ragged chalk cliffs which forms such a delightful background and accentuates the blue of the water. They pass *Creston* (doubtless Preston) beach and stop opposite *Ringsworth Shore*—suggestively Ringstead.

The action now moves inland and our interest is claimed by *Knapwater House*. This was probably suggested by Kingston Maurward House, which stands in a magnificently timbered park containing some fine specimens of lime and other deciduous trees. The house was built by a cousin of William Pitt at the end of the eighteenth century. When George III. was once paying a visit there, he is reported to have been asked by Pitt what he thought of the house, and to have replied: "Only brick, Pitt, only brick!" The result of this criticism was soon apparent, for Pitt had the whole house encased with a shell of stone, fixed to the brickwork with copper clamps. We read that "the house was regularly and substantially built of clean grey free-stone throughout," a description we verify when we examine it (180).

If we can obtain permission to explore in Kingston Park we shall find much to interest us. The house, which has a stately, dignified appearance, stands on an eminence, the ground sloping away from it in all directions ; a delightful lawn on the south side leads down to the lake, a fine sheet of water margined by timber trees and an undergrowth of rushes, reeds, and irises, beautiful indeed in spring when their masses of yellow flowers reflect the sunlight. On the water are mallards, coots, moorhens, and little grebes, sailing about among the herbage and disappearing mysteriously at the first indication of danger. If we turn eastward along the path that skirts the water, we shall soon see on our left hand a summer house—evidently the one which suggested "the Fane, built . . . in the form of a

180.—Kingston Maurward House.

181.—The Summer House or Temple, Kingston Park.

Grecian temple." (It is in fact called "The Temple" to this day) (181). Near it is the water-wheel (now closed in) giving out its continuous, monotonous throbbing. A little farther, and the path winds through thick undergrowth and emerges at the end of the lake, where the water empties itself in a cascade. From this spot we catch a glimpse of the old Manor-House—recently illustrated in an architectural work on Tudor mansions —which stands to us for the building where Manston lived (182); and as we walk towards it we are struck with a sound that is realistically suggestive of the duet which greeted Cytherea's ears on her arrival—a blended sound of the waterfall and the pumping engine.

The old building now before us has obviously seen better days. It belonged originally to the Grey family, from whom it passed with the estates to the Pitts by the marriage of George Pitt to Laura, only child and heiress of Audley Grey. The story tells us of the restoration of this old Tudor building, which had fallen so low as to be "contained under three gables and a cross roof behind." It has passed through many changes since that time, but even to-day it exhibits a certain old grandeur which speaks to us of its past.

On the side of the lake remote from the house is a public footpath leading from Dorchester to Bock-hampton, and from it we obtain an excellent view of *Knapwater House*, with the lake in the foreground, and the slope of greensward behind it in the middle distance. Perhaps it was on this path that Spring-rove was supposed to be standing when he wished Cytherea farewell and their hands met across the stream. There are many associations connected with this path, for it figures in the poem entitled "The Dead Quire," and repeatedly in "Under the Green-wood Tree."

Peakhill Cottage was a representation of a cottage standing on the high ground behind the old Manor-House ; its thatch roof still remains, but there is little else now to commend it.

182.—THE OLD MANOR-HOUSE, KINGSTON PARK.

183.—TOLPUDDLE CHURCH AND THE MANOR FARM.

Carriford Village, Carriford Road Station, the *Three Tranters Inn*, and the Rectory, must all be regarded as imaginary creations, although certain features show them as suggested by portions of West Stafford, Puddletown, etc. The church we may perhaps regard as drawn more or less from the church at Puddletown, or that at Stafford; but this latter was thoroughly restored in 1897 and a chancel added. Over the porch is the date 1640, referring probably to the time at which it was rebuilt. The whole village has seen considerable alteration; many of these changes produced marked effects on the residents—a fact which may be exemplified by a quotation from the lips of an old bailiff who once lived in Stafford. He is reported to have said: "When Reggie's gone and Johnnie's gone and George is gone —good-bye Stafford." Reggie referred to Canon Reginald Smith, Johnnie to the squire, and George to himself. A reason, however, for returning to Puddletown as the probable original is that, a few years before the date of the story, a row of thatched cottages opposite the church was burnt down precisely in the manner described.

The village of Tolpuddle seems to have suggested *Tolchurch* to our author. Owen was supposed to have gone there to superintend the restoration of the church, and to have lodged meanwhile at the farm-house near by. Tolpuddle is a picturesque, old-world village standing on the river Pydel—a Saxon word which gives its name to many of the villages which lie on its banks, the word being spelt in a variety of ways. The church— decidedly over-" restored "—is built of flints and stone and is of Early English and Perpendicular periods. Close to it is the farm-house which served as the house in which the fictitious Owen and Cytherea resided (183).

Anglebury suggests Wareham, more or less. It is the station only which concerns us in this story, for here Manston is supposed to wait for the *Tolchurch* postman. We see them plodding along, stopping here and there to deliver letters, and finally reaching *Tolchurch*.

Casterbridge has been so fully explored when we were concerned with "The Mayor of Casterbridge," that it need not detain us here. We may, however, mention that the *County Bank* was figured from a building which has now been demolished, as also has the old county gaol.

CHAPTER II

"THE HAND OF ETHELBERTA"

(*A Comedy in Chapters*)

THE landscapes which form the environment in this
lively book are to be discovered chiefly in Dorset, or
South Wessex.   The towns which figure have become
fashionable seaside resorts since the date of the story,
and consequently we must be prepared to find considerable alteration in the places described.   The
action commences at *Anglebury*—approximately Wareham—where we are introduced to that "old and well-
appointed Inn," the " Red Lion," a building of imposing
appearance standing at the cross-roads in the centre of
the town (184).   This inn receives repeated mention
and forms a convenient halting-place or half-way house
between Swanage and Bournemouth.   Wareham is a
sleepy little town—in fact, it used to be said that the
inhabitants only got up once a week, on market days!
The town is almost surrounded by earthen walls ;
whether these are of Saxon or British construction is
open to question, though it is generally supposed they
are pre-Saxon.   A local legend tells us that they were
built to imprison the cuckoo, which was always supposed to arrive on Wareham Fair Day ; and it is
alleged that the townspeople, annoyed because the
bird did not stay within the town limits, determined
to construct earthen walls to shut it in.   This was
accordingly done, and the following year the bird
duly arrived on the proper day, but soon flew away,

184.—WAREHAM.

185.—ST. MARTIN'S CHURCH, WAREHAM.

just skimming over the top of the wall; whereupon one of the builders said: "Ther' now, if we'd a-builded they walls zix inches higher he 'ouldn' never have a-vleed away."

The town was occupied from very early times, and in 876 was held by the Danes. There was once a priory here, said to have been founded by St. Aldhelm, Bishop of Sherborne, about 701. There was also a castle prior to the Norman Conquest, the site being still visible. Wareham was accounted a borough in Domesday Book. The port was important in the Middle Ages, and during the French war in 1334 it was required to furnish four ships. Of the churches, that of St. Martin, exhibiting Saxon and four other styles of architecture, is the most interesting (185).

We read of Ethelberta starting from the inn for a country walk with, according to the hostler, "a clane-washed face, her hair in buckle." She pauses for a while on the bridge spanning the Froom, and then crosses the railway and follows the right-hand road. Presently she is distracted by the sight of a wild duck pursued by a hawk, and follows the birds across the heath until she comes close to "a whitely shining oval of still water, looking amid the swathy level of the heath like a hole through to a nether sky." We may recognise the spot in its likeness to Morden Decoy, some three miles from Wareham to the north-west. Here she meets with Julian, who was on his way to *Flychett*—suggestively Lytchett Minster (186).

Sandbourne, which we have decided to regard as the counterfeit of Bournemouth, and the somewhat distant tract of water-meadow, marsh, and heathland —known in the book as *Sandbourne Moor*, and brought rather nearer to the town than in reality—forms the next background. In this town of mushroom growth we cannot hope to find the actual houses which served our author for models; the moor, too, has now been built upon to such an extent that its old-time characteristics are scarcely traceable.

186.—LYTCHETT HEATH.

187.—THE OLD MILL-POND, SWANAGE.

243

"Three or four miles out of the town" and "overlooking a wide sheet of sea" stood *Wyndway House*. The description strongly suggests Upton House, and a good view of it can be had from the railway between Hamworthy and Poole stations. It is here that Julian and his sister are represented playing for the dancing. On their journey back to *Sandbourne* they catch a glimpse of Ethelberta and Picotee walking along the shore of a sandy nook, doubtless on the harbour shore towards the Sandbanks, which the road would have overlooked.

Rookington Park is described as "abounding with timber older and finer than that of any other spot in the neighbourhood." From this we are inclined to place it as Hern Court, near Christchurch.

The house in which Ethelberta lived for a time with her mother and the children was the lodge of a newly-built house on the borders of the *Great Forest* —our author's pseudonym for the New Forest—known as *Arrowthorne Lodge*. It appears to be meant for one of the modern mansions in the neighbourhood of the wood called "The Earldoms," on the north side of the New Forest, between Romsey and Fordingbridge. There are, however, no distinctive features described by which we may recognise the individual mansion.

Such scenes as are supposed to take place in ordinary London houses we may ignore. Cripplegate Church is of course easily found, but the houses mentioned are too vague to be discoverable.

Farnfield is approximately Farnborough, where Neigh had his "little place" and where Ethelberta in a moment of rash enthusiasm went to "spy out the land." The actual spot is naturally not to be found now, after years of building, but is quite typical of grounds when laid out before the mansion is erected.

The action again brings us back to South Wessex, with *Knollsea* as the background. This is virtually Swanage, once a mere fishing village, now a rising watering-place. The streets are sadly disfigured with newly erected buildings of a blatant style of architecture which utterly spoils the ancient picturesqueness of the place. Our author describes it as "a seaside village lying snug within two headlands as between a finger and thumb," a description which we find particularly apposite. The most interesting portion of the town nowadays centres at the old church, close to which is the mill, and several stone-built and stone-roofed cottages—all congruous with the date when Ethelberta is imagined to have visited the little town (187). We note with regret the widowerhood of "Old Harry," one of the several rocky pinnacles which jut out at the Foreland. They are formed of chalk and flints, and the sea is constantly eating out the foundations. "Old Harry's wife"—a companion rock—subsided from this cause, falling down one night during a terrific gale—well remembered in Swanage from the fact that the life-boat was wrecked the same night. These two rocky pillars are known in Studland, a village just round the Foreland, by opposite titles, the Studland folk maintaining it is Old Harry himself who has gone, his wife who remains. The differing opinions lead to interesting remarks from the two sets of thinkers! The clock-tower, which stands between the pier and the coast-guard station, stood once on London Bridge; but a new and not too appropriate canopy takes the place of the original spire. The façade of the Town Hall was brought from Mercers' Hall and was designed by Wren. The cottage in which Ethelberta is supposed to have stayed with her brothers and sisters has been altered into a more modern structure, and now passes by the name of "Durlston Cottage."

Let us track Ethelberta when she goes on her memorable excursion to *Corvesgate Castle*, the counterfeit presentment of Corfe Castle. She starts along "a path by the shore . . . and thence up the steep crest of land opposite." We see her, after resting for a while, "turning to the left along the lofty ridge which ran inland, the country on each side lay beneath her like a map . . . through a huge cemetery of barrows, containing human dust from prehistoric times." We have little difficulty in recognising Nine-barrow Down, where tradition says nine kings or chieftains were killed in one great battle against the Romans, and were buried, each in one of the nine barrows. We are told of the strange diversity of country which greeted Ethelberta's eyes on both sides of the ridge. The long high down seems to form a line of demarcation separating two very dissimilar types of landscape. On the northern side of the hill is a vast stretch of heath, and beyond it the serrated margin of Poole Harbour, with its islands, some treed, others bare, and in the distance the cliffs of Bournemouth. On the southern side we are greeted by the Purbeck Hills, and behind them the open sea. The different aspects are accentuated by the contrasts in lighting which the opposite sides of the hill obtain.

We will follow Ethelberta as she walks along the top of the ridge and descends into the village. In imagination we watch her as she "crossed the bridge over the moat and rode under the first archway into the outer ward . . . ascending the green incline and through another arch into the second ward." Then, after a further climb on foot, she is among the "windy corridors and mildewed dungeons," wherein Peter the Hermit, Edward II., and King John were once prisoners. The history of this ancient castle is too long to enter into now; it is scarcely necessary to say that after many vicissitudes it was blown up at the time of the Commonwealth, since when it has remained in ruins (188).

Enkworth Court by its ascribed position suggests Encombe; it was the seat of Lord Mountclere in the story, and the description of its site at least answers fairly well to that of Encombe House. But as to the building itself, the reader needs to be reminded of the

188.—CORFE CASTLE.

189.—PETER'S FINGER INN, LYTCHETT MINSTER.

remark in my Introduction, that realities form only a peg for the depicted places to hang on, these latter existing nowhere outside the books. Thus the marvellous staircase said to be contained in the present building is either imported from elsewhere or is a pure figment of the author's imagination.

Melchester, representing Salisbury, figures so prominently in the book entitled " Jude the Obscure " that we need now merely notice the " Red Lion " and the " White Hart," both well-known hostels bearing their legitimate names. It was in the Cathedral close that Ethelberta is supposed to tell Christopher of her intended marriage ; and inside the Cathedral she is reconciled to Mountclere and promises to marry him on a definite date.

This leads up to a wild crisis in her life, and we read of her brothers, accompanied by the brother of Mountclere, trying to prevent the marriage. We may watch them, imaginatively, leaving London and arriving at *Sandbourne*, and we may follow them in their abortive attempt to reach *Knollsea* by steamer and their subsequent return to *Sandbourne*. Thence they determine to post. First crossing *Sandbourne Moor* — where Picotee had so often met Julian earlier in the history— passing *Wyndway House*, leaving *Havenpool*—practically Poole—on their left hand, its "eyelets of light winking to them in the distance from under a nebulous brow of pale haze," they come to *Flychett*, that "trumpery small bit of a village " which we have held as being more or less akin to Lytchett Minster. Here they rest the horses at the inn called " Peter's Finger " —a house which still exhibits a swinging sign characteristic of its name, a corruption of *St. Peter ad Vincula* (189). In due course they reach *Anglebury*, where once again we see our old friend Hostler John coming from under the "shadowy archway" of the "Red Lion" and viewing the "mighty ekkypage" bowling towards him at that early, "purblinking" hour. With fresh horses they continue their harum-scarum journey

190.—St. Mary's Church, Swanage.

191.—The Castle Inn, Corfe Castle.

to *Corvesgate Castle*, where they climb the steep ascent leading to *Little Enkworth*—perhaps Kingston Village —and pass on to *Enkworth Court*.   Frustrated here, we see them hurrying towards *Knollsea* and reaching the church with its "square unembattled tower" too late to prevent the marriage (190).

The action goes back to *Enkworth Court*, and then to the "Castle Inn" at *Corvesgate Castle*.   This inn, passing under the same name to-day, stands at the end of the street nearest to Swanage and still retains much of its old-time appearance (191).   With Christopher we pay a last visit to *Enkworth Court* and catch a glimpse of Ethelberta—"her bonnet, her shoulders, her hair—but no more."   Then going by steamer from *Knollsea* we pass "Old Harry" and reach *Sandbourne*. There are numbers of "Fir-top villas" at Bournemouth now, and it is useless to attempt to isolate the particular one from which the house in the story is drawn.

CHAPTER III

" A LAODICEAN "

THE townlet of Dunster provides us with a facsimile of the background against which most of the action in this story takes place; but we must not attempt so close a comparison of the actual with the factitious as we have achieved in some other instances. That Dunster Castle served in a great measure as the model for *Stancy Castle* we may be certain; but if we approach it to-day, our minds filled with a picture of the building as it appeared to George Somerset, we shall feel constrained to admit that certain features and details must have been supplied by our author, either from imagination or from the reminiscences of other architectural piles.

The name Dunster prepares us to some extent for the situation of the castle. Tor means tower; dun means hill; and hence we are not surprised to find an almost precipitous hill, clothed with grand old trees, from which the richly coloured stone towers and parapets rise against the skyline (192). The history of the castle carries us a long way back in time. When Edward the Confessor was king, Dunster Castle was held by Aluric, but William the Conqueror made it over to William de Mohun. During the Parliamentary wars its politics changed rapidly: first it declared for the Parliament, afterwards for King Charles; then it was besieged for several months by Cromwell's forces, to whom it finally surrendered. In 1376 it was purchased by the ancestors of the present owner.

251

As we enter from the north the little town of Dunster—called *Markton* in the novel—the castle occupies a very commanding position, towering above the houses (193). The main street is exceptionally wide, and near its centre stands the old Yarn Market, an octagonal wooden building with wide overhanging eaves and eight little dormer-windows (194). It is crowned by a lantern, from which rises a weather-vane with the initials G. L., and bearing the date of 1647. On the left-hand side is a remarkably fine old inn—the " Luttrell Arms "—containing many details of archæological interest (195). In all probability our author's conception of the " Lord Quantock Arms " was derived from this. There is an atmosphere of mediævalism pervading the little town ; no insidious modern innovations have been allowed to creep in ; and we seem to be able freely to conjecture from its present appearance what it must have been like two or three centuries back in time.

As I have hinted above, we shall not be able to plod in the footsteps of the actors in this story as we have been able to do in the case of some of the other Wessex Novels, for there is not that exactitude of description regarding the backgrounds which is such a noticeable feature in the majority of the books. For instance, the little hamlet of *Sleeping Green*, where Somerset at first was staying, does not bear sufficient description to warrant us in identifying it with any particular village to be discovered in the immediate neighbourhood of Dunster, though it suggests either Carhampton or Withycombe. *Toneborough*, a barrack town, one may define pretty safely to be an imaginative portrait of Taunton, a town which, in some of the other stories, appears also under the same name. But the description places it some dozen miles nearer to *Stancy Castle* than it actually is.

To return again to *Markton*, or Dunster (called a village sometimes in the novel). It is in the church here—a most interesting one—that the family tombs of

192.—Dunster Castle.

193.—Dunster Village and Castle.

253

194.—Dunster Village.

195.—The Luttrell Arms Hotel, Dunster.

254

the De Stancys are imagined to have stood (196). The style is mainly that of the fifteenth century, though in the archway of the west door we find a good illustration of Norman work. It stands on the site of an earlier Saxon church, but no tangible evidence of the older fabric is discoverable. A beautifully carved oak

196.—The Church, Dunster.

screen traverses the entire width of the building, and there are many interesting monuments to be seen. From the belfry the chimes ring out every four hours. On Sunday we may hear *O Rest in the Lord!* On Monday, *Drink to me only!* On Tuesday, *Home, sweet Home!* On Wednesday, *Disposer supreme!* On Thursday, *The Blue Bells of Scotland!* On

Friday, *Old 113th!* On Saturday, *Hark, hark, my Soul!* A curious medley of tunes! In the churchyard wall is a wide-arched recess, generally said to mark the site of the stocks, and in the rectory garden may be seen the ruins of a Benedictine Priory.

Close behind the little town is a high hill called Grabhurst, or Grabbist, and from the summit a magnificent bird's-eye view of the surrounding country is obtained. The beautiful Vale of Avill, Dunkery Beacon (scene of the Ballad-tragedy entitled "The Sacrilege," published in *The Fortnightly Review* in 1911), the country from North Hill to Watchet, the Bristol Channel, with Holm Islands standing out strongly, and behind it the line of the Welsh coast, mountains rising back, tier upon tier. Right under our feet clusters the townlet of Dunster, guarded by the castle on one side and Conegar Tower on the other. A huge deer park surrounds the castle, and through it wanders a sparkling stream.

The few details given above form but a meagre description of the backgrounds of the story, but the present writer fears to stray beyond the bounds of veracity into the realms of imagination.

PART IV

POETICAL WORKS

CHAPTER I

"WESSEX POEMS"

WE are told in the preface that "the pieces are in a large degree dramatic or personative in conception." Nevertheless, many of them are supplied with settings drawn with that realistic touch which we have come to look on as an integral part of our author's work. Just as poetry is a more subtle mode of self-expression than prose, so in like manner we find the scenery of these poems sketched in with a few deft strokes, of course less detailed than in the novels.

"San Sebastian" has for its setting the *Ivel Way*, that old Roman road which led through Bath until it reached Ilchester, where it branched through Yeovil to Dorchester, and on the other fork led to Exeter. There is a reference to the *Hintock Maypole*, which brings our minds back to the story of "The Woodlanders." Maypole-dancing is now almost extinct, though an occasional Wessex village may be seen where the Maypole still rears itself on the green— notably at the village of Shillingstone, between Wimborne and Blandford. Round-the-Maypole was once one of the most popular of the Morris or Moorish dances, and was introduced into England from Spain in the time of Edward III.

THE BURGHERS

We find the scene laid in Dorchester, the *Casterbridge* of the novels. Here, in the old High Street, the friends are supposed to meet (197). The hour is aptly determined by the words :

The sun had wheeled from Grey's to Dammer's Crest ;

that is to say, from Grey's Bridge or Grey's Wood to the eastward, very familiar to us in " Under the Greenwood Tree," to the apex of Damer's Hill, which lies just outside the town on the Bridport Road, close to the barn which we inspected in "The Mayor of Casterbridge." The house described as the " Pleasaunce hard by Glyd'path Rise " is the same house which we have ascribed to Lucetta in the last-mentioned book, and known to-day as Colliton House. " Three hours past curfew" fixes the point of time with accuracy, for St. Peter's Church still announces the curfew nightly at eight o'clock.

In imagination we pass down the High Street in the still hours when the town is wrapped in sleep, and turn down the narrow road called Glyde Path Road. Before us stands Colliton House, looking grey and ghastly in the faint light, and close beside it the ancient gateway with the grinning mask forming its keystone. To appreciate fully the depth and feeling of the poem we need to visit the scene at such an hour, to view it by the faint light of the stars, rather than by the strenuous light of the sun.

THE ALARM

Here we are taken into the atmosphere of, and over some of the ground traversed in, "The Trumpet-Major" and "The Dynasts." The homestead "in a ferny byway" lay not far from Upper Bockhampton, and here we picture the volunteer bidding his wife farewell ere he takes the road for " Royal George's Town " —an obvious description of Weymouth. Before he starts he bids his wife be prepared to journey to *Kingsbere*—the townlet we have seen to be Bere Regis —should rumour reach her of Napoleon's landing. It

197.—HIGH WEST STREET, DORCHESTER.

198.—MAIDEN CASTLE, DORCHESTER.

261

was, in fact, the spot mentioned in the Government Orders of the date for the retreat of the women and children.

This was on the day following the kindling of the beacons, and as he journeys onward he sees "The Barrow - Beacon burning — burning low," on Rain-barrows—an ancient burial-place which bulks largely in "The Return of the Native" and also in "The Dynasts." We will follow in his footsteps. When he reaches the river Froom he hesitates whether to proceed or to turn back ; but his mind is made up for him by watching the flight of the bird he releases from the river weeds, which bears over the river, crosses *Durnover Great-Field* (Fordington Field), and continues due southward. Then he pursues his way, passing *Mai-Don* (198), and climbing Ridgeway Hill. Maiden Castle we shall examine more closely in "Time's Laughing-stocks," and the Ridgeway when we are exploring the scenery of "The Dynasts."

HER DEATH AND AFTER

Here we are still in *Casterbridge*. Right at the top of High West Street, facing directly down the street, is a solidly built house known as Top o' Town. It was from this house that "her tenement" was drawn. The *Western Wall* has received mention in "The Mayor of Casterbridge," where it is called *Chalk Walk*—another and less-used name for Colliton Walk. In the *Field of the Tombs* we recognise the cemetery on the Weymouth Road—just beyond the *Cirque of the Gladiators*, or Maumbury Rings, lately examined by the antiquaries.

THE DANCE AT THE PHŒNIX

The "Phœnix" is one of the old-time hostelries of Dorchester (though with a new frontage) and stands in High East Street, nearly opposite the

199.—The Phœnix Hotel, Dorchester.

200.—The Gateway, Basing House.

263

THE WESSEX OF THOMAS HARDY

" Three Mariners "—a familiar spot in "The Mayor of Casterbridge" (199). "The Faynix" has always been favoured by the soldiery at the barracks for their convivial gatherings. Various other features mentioned in this poem have also come before us in the last-named book, but *Standfast Bridge* occurs here for the first time. We shall find it by passing down the length of Mill Street.

CASTERBRIDGE CAPTAINS

Here we need only visit the church of All Saints, to which our author refers in "the ancient aisle." The names said to be carved on the seat-back were there before the reseating, and at this distance of time there may be no harm in giving them as J. B. Lock, T. G. Besant, and J. Logan.

MY CICELY

"The ancient West Highway" refers to the old Roman Road leading from London to Exeter. Let us follow the wayfarer in imagination. First we hear of him passing "The House of Long-sieging." This, the well-known Basing House, near the village of Old Basing, is now in complete ruin, but was once a famous mansion. During the time of the first Civil War it was fortified for the king by John Paulett, who is said to have engraved the words *Aimez Loyauté* on every pane of glass in the house. It stood a succession of blockades between 1643 and 1645, and on the 14th of October in the latter year it was stormed by Oliver Cromwell himself. During the attack it caught fire and was burned down, the very ruins being razed by order of the Parliament. There is little now to mark its existence except a portion of the gateway and some interior walls (200).

Next, the rider is said to come in sight of Salisbury Cathedral, disguised as the fair fane of "Poore's

264

olden Episcopal See." "The Stour-bordered Forum," through which he passes, speaks to us of Blandford with its old-time market-place. It is the *Shottsford-Forum* of the novels. *Weatherbury Castle*, another wayside object, has already come before us in the novel entitled "Two on a Tower," where it forms part of a composite scene. Thence he passes through *Casterbridge*, in sight of *Maidon*—the finest earthwork in this country, already referred to—until he reaches "The Hill-fortress of Eggar," and leaves "Square Pummerie" (Poundbury Camp) to the north. In *Eggar* we recognise Eggardon, another fine example of British earth-castles with an almost impregnable position, and commanding a wide outlook over the surrounding country. In due course he reaches *Exonbury*—a city practically conterminous with Exeter. "The famed Lions-Three" stands about ten miles back from the city on the Taunton Road.

FRIENDS BEYOND

Here the little church of Stinsford comes before us, though of course in the old guise in which we see it at the time of "Under the Greenwood Tree" (201).

IN A WOOD

If we ramble through the *Hintock Woods*, familiar to us in the book entitled "The Woodlanders," we shall find the country which formed the setting for this poem (202).

THE IMPERCIPIENT

It was during a service in Salisbury Cathedral that our author was impressed and inspired to compare the various thoughts that seemed to echo through the aisles. When we were examining the backgrounds in "Jude the Obscure" we inspected the Cathedral more closely.

201.—STINSFORD CHURCH.

202.—WOODS NEAR HILLFIELD.

266

"WESSEX POEMS"

At an Inn

At the George Inn at Winchester these verses were written ; but beyond stating this as a crude fact there is nothing further to dilate on.

The Slow Nature

This poem brings the Froom Valley before our eyes—the valley which occurs so often as a background in " Tess of the d'Urbervilles." In *Moreford Rise* we find a fictitious presentment of a hill close to Moreton Village, in the direction of Winfrith. " Far Egdon-side " and " the rippling Froom " indicate at once a locality not remote from *Talbothays*.

In a Eweleaze near Weatherbury

There are many spots near Puddletown which might serve for the scenery in this poem, but to those who know the district well it seems to point to a particular grassy down known as Coomb. This field is on the road from Puddletown towards *Egdon Heath*, and was at one time a favourite spot for village festivities.

CHAPTER II

"POEMS OF THE PAST AND THE PRESENT"

THE SOULS OF THE SLAIN

ALL in harmony with the weird, profound thoughts which fill this poem is the wild, forlorn aspect of Nature at Portland Bill, its background (203). To the solitary seer who muses here on the rocky headland comes the phantasmagorical procession of "frameless souls," and we have but to visit the spot when the sombre shades of darkness are closing down upon it to picture to ourselves that self-same crowd of hurrying spirits. We may then readily imagine them flitting in and out the dark caverns or hovering over the opalescent sheen which marks the Race — out there to the south-east, towards the Shambles. In summer-time, by daylight, the rocks take on a less forbidding aspect and the sea is in a calm mood. But in winter, and especially at dusk, when the waves are piling themselves on each other and angrily lashing the rocks, to fall back disappointed, yet, in fancy, not disheartened — then is the time to enter into our author's imaginary picture and comprehend somewhat of its significance.

THE MOTHER MOURNS

In the western portion of *Egdon Heath* the highest horizon line is backed by the dense trees of Yellowham Woods. Deep dark recesses are to be found in these

203.—THE PULPIT ROCK, PORTLAND BILL.

204.—ATHELHAMPTON HALL.

woods, spots where the sunlight rarely enters in summer because of the thick leaf-curtains, where squirrels leap from branch to branch and the shy woodpecker finds a home. Here is the setting for the present poem, in the *Yalbury Woods*, already familiar to us as forming one of the backgrounds in " Under the Greenwood Tree."

THE LACKING SENSE

The background here is Waddon Vale, that deep valley running from Upwey towards Abbotsbury. High above it on the northern side is Blagdon, or Blackdown, whence the Hardy Monument rises skywards.

THE WELL-BELOVED

This poem, it should be noted, has no connection with the novel bearing the same title. Its setting (in the Wessex Edition) is at Jordan Hill, near Weymouth —the ancient Roman station Clavinium—where there are the remains of a Roman temple, tessellated pavements, and other relics of the Roman occupation. *Jordon Grove* speaks to us of Preston Vale, a well-wooded depression hard by. Artistic Roman pottery has been found in large quantities hereabouts, and good examples of Samian ware.

I NEED NOT GO

There is nothing for us to remark here except the prime fact that Stinsford Churchyard holds the tomb in which *She* lies.

LONG PLIGHTED

Again the country of Yellowham Woods comes before us, with its surrounding of *Egdon Heath*.

"POEMS OF THE PAST AND PRESENT"

The Dame of Athelhall

Athelhall is a presentment of Athelhampton, a magnificent example of Tudor building with some evidences of earlier work, and one of the oldest and most beautiful in the county (204). It is traditionally said to have been erected on the site of a castle, once a stronghold of King Athelstan. In recent years it has been considerably altered and enlarged.

The Levelled Churchyard

Although this poem might with justice refer to many of our churchyards, the particular one in our author's mind was evidently that of Wimborne, where ducks and drakes were played with the headstones at the "Restoration" to a truly amazing extent.

The Lost Pyx

Cerne Abbas, under its slight disguise of *Abbot's Cernel*, figures as the first locality in this poem. It is inside the ancient abbey that the priest is imagined to see his first vision.

Cernel's Abbey was at one time in a thriving condition, but little remains to-day to testify to its vigour, though it might be reconstructed from the numerous fragments of mouldings scattered about. It is said to have been founded by Alwald to commemorate his brother, St. Edmund the Martyr, once king of East Anglia. The gate-house, bearing the shields of the Earl of Cornwall, the Abbey Barn, and certain features in the Abbey House and outbuildings alone remain as reminiscences of the past (205). Cerne bears the imprint of having been once a busy town, and history assures us that it was at one time quite a considerable place, containing tanneries and a brewery of no mean size. It used to be celebrated as the dearest-rented

205.—Remains of Cerne Abbey.

206.—Cerne Abbas.

place in all Dorset (206). The church is Perpendicular, with a fine tower and an interesting wood screen kept in fair preservation. On a hill-side close to the village is the "Cerne Giant," a rudely cut figure nearly two hundred feet in length, and of what origin we have no accurate knowledge. Many are the legendary stories attaching to it, and various superstitions still linger in the neighbourhood in connection therewith. Perhaps the most popular theory is that in mediæval times a giant did actually live in the district, and frequently raided the farmers' stockyards in the adjoining Black-moor Vale ; that on one occasion, after an exceptionally heavy repast, he lay down to sleep on the hill-side, where the villagers discovered him, fastened him to the ground with ropes and pegs, and then slew him and traced his outline by cutting away the grass. By most antiquarians it is thought to represent the work of mediæval monks from the abbey below ; but probably its origin is in a more remote past. A small earthwork near the church is attributed to Celtic residence.

In imagination we may picture the priest rising up and starting forth to shrive the dying man, struggling through the storm until he reaches the spot called Cross-in-Hand (207). Of all weird, lonesome spots few can compete with the bleak hill-top whereon this mysterious pillar rears itself from the grassy downland. Its origin is as unknown as that of the Giant of Cerne. It may have been a cross, possessed of sacred significance ; it may have represented a boundary mark ; or, as others affirm, it may have been a pagan monument. Locally it is also called Crossy-hand, from the fact that the figure of a woman with her hands crossed was once discernible. But all signs of carving have become obliterated now, and not a vestige remains of the basin which once crowned its apex.

The present topographer was informed by an old gipsy woman that it was a wishing-stone, and that any individual who placed his hand upon the stone and registered a wish would invariably find it come true. There were certain conditions necessary, and certain precautions to be taken, but into these we must not enter now. Suffice it that this has been put to the test on more than one occasion, with results that fully

207.—CROSS-IN-HAND.

justified the gipsy woman's prediction. Absence of accurate knowledge is often termed superstition— there we will leave the matter.

This stone comes before us when we follow Tess on her journey from *Flintcomb-Ash* to *Emminster* and back, on which occasion she is represented as swearing an oath with her hand on the stone at Alec d'Urberville's dictation. From the vicinity of the stone there spreads out before us a wide view, embracing almost the whole of the Blackmoor Vale, with, in clear weather, a glimpse of the Bristol Channel as well as the English Channel. High-Stoy, Bubb-Down, and other landmarks are visible, and beneath us nestle the hamlets and villages known in "The Woodlanders" as the *Hintocks*. The spot may be reached by taking the road leading from Minterne to Evershot, or by a drive in the contrary direction from Evershot station.

Tess's Lament

Here we are recalled to the time when Tess and Angel Clare parted, after their mutual confession regarding the past. There is the atmosphere of the valley of the Froom, where lie the "Great Dairies," and amongst them *Talbothays*, where she sojourned for so long, and whither her mind now turned with regretful longing. But we have already explored this section of the country when viewing the backgrounds against which the several scenes in Tess's life-history stand out—the whole story is vividly recalled to our mind by the verses now before us.

CHAPTER III

" THE DYNASTS "

FOR obvious reasons there will be no attempt made in this Guide-book to conduct the reader over the Continental scenery which forms the bewildering variety of theatres for the huge Epic-Drama that lie outside England and its surrounding waters. The action of the drama in this country alone will take us over a wide stretch of land, and we shall revisit certain places which we have already examined in some of the previous novels and poems. The fresh features introduced demand our interest, and we shall look on them from new standpoints and in different lights.

The first scene of the first act of " The Dynasts " is not mentioned by any distinctive name, but its description enables us to recognise it as having been planned and drawn from the summit of Ridgeway Hill, midway between Dorchester and Weymouth (208). We have visited the spot when with our friends from *Overcombe* we climbed over the downs to see King George and his retinue pass by. This time we are drawn hither in order that we may overhear the converse of the stage-coach passengers in the pause at the top of the hill.

If at the present day we approach the hill from Dorchester we shall notice, just before the actual summit is reached, a track on the right-hand side. This was the old road, and it passed over the ridge and descended somewhat abruptly into the village of

276

Upwey, where its junction with the newer road is readily seen. It is with the older track that we are concerned. It has not been mended for many years, and portions of it are now covered with grass. As we commence the descent a wonderful panorama lies before us. The Isle of Portland rises out of the sea, looking grim and forbidding, and between it and the Ridgeway the roofs of Weymouth glitter in the sunlight, while myriad sparkles are reflected from the bay and the lake-like inlet known as the Backwater. On our left hand lies Bincombe Down, its rounded barrows "like the bosoms of an amazon" standing clearly out against the skyline. To the right of Weymouth we catch glimpses of the Chesil Beach and the long sweeping curve which forms the shore-line of West Bay, or *Dead-man's Bay*. It is not until we descend lower, however, that other features, now hidden by the Ridgeway itself, are uncovered.

The word ridge is here used in its purest meaning. Its course is marked by innumerable barrows, and a walk along the *rucke*, or back, from this point to the monument which tops Blackdown will repay us with a view not easily equalled in any part of Wessex.

It is while we listen in imagination to the discourse of the passengers that we learn of the proposed visit of the Court to " King George's Watering-place " (the periphrase used in this drama for Weymouth)—and thus the fact of there being "a deal of traffic over Ridgeway " is accounted for. At that date the minds of all who dwelt near the coast were perturbed with thoughts of Napoleon's arrival ; and much speculation was rife regarding the actual spot at which the landing would be accomplished. This daily and hourly dread is vividly brought before us in " The Trumpet-Major," as well as in the poem entitled " The Alarm," already alluded to.

In the fourth scene of the second act we are on Bincombe Down hard by—the *Overcombe Down* of " The Trumpet-Major," and the same background as

208.—At the Apex of Ridgeway Hill.

209.—Bincombe Down.

278

served for the short story entitled "The Melancholy
Hussar of the German Legion." Our first impression
on reaching the top of the hill is its changelessness.
Here, among the barrows wherein our ancestors or
their enemies lie sleeping, is a slice of the world which
seems never to have been tampered with by human
agency ; we imagine it to have been thus through
countless ages, and it is difficult to think of it as ever
becoming other than it is to-day (209).

The name Bincombe is supposed to be derived
from the English-Saxon word Binan-Comb, meaning
the inside dell, and doubtless refers to the contour of
the hill. In the description of the scene (using the
word in its oldest and purest sense as denoting a
platform) we read : "The down commands a wide
view over the English Channel in front of it, including
the popular Royal watering-place (Weymouth) with
the Isle of Slingers (Portland) and its roadstead,
where men-of-war and frigates are anchored," etc. If
we will examine this description in the light of to-day
we shall find it true to the letter ; excepting that the
old men-of-war and frigates are now represented by
cruisers, Dreadnoughts, and torpedo boats.

This is where the review takes place ; the king,
now in residence at *Gloucester Lodge*, rides up on
horseback to witness it, and his presence is viewed
with consternation by some of his loyal subjects, who
fear lest he should fall into Napoleon's clutches ; for
one of the spectators declares : "Gloucester Lodge
could be surrounded, and George and Charlotte carried
off before he could put on his hat, or she her red cloak
and pattens !" The review—historically accurate—
was a monster one of the first years of the nineteenth
century ; the line is said to have extended three miles.
The plateau is sufficient to accommodate a vast con-
course of people ; its space is divided here and there
by stone walls composed either of thin upright slabs
or of rubble stone built with dry joints.

The down—so little altered in its general aspect—

has seen many a military camp pitched and struck upon it since then ; its surface has been scored by the hoofs of gaily caparisoned chargers, as, earlier, by the foot of uncivilised man ; but it probably never looked so gay or was so thickly populated as in the days when George III. was king, and when the dread Napoleon, "that arch-enemy of mankind," was daily expected to run his flat-bottomed boats on the beach that lay in view of its summit.

Standing here, more than 500 feet above the sea, with the aid of a glass we can make out a large number of the spots in the surrounding country which figure in the Wessex Poems and Novels. The *Isle of Slingers* lies, "like a whale on the sea," due south of us ; Hope Cove and the Beal and the Race are hidden from us, and only the Castletown heights, with the fort showing above, are conspicuous. Between us and the Island lies *Creston Shore* ; almost at our feet is the little church of Bincombe, marking the resting-place of Phyllis Grove and Matthius Tina and his comrade. Sweeping westward with the sun, the narrow neck of pebbles that connects Portland with the mainland comes in, forming a portion of the Chesil Beach, and flanked on the east by Portland Roads, on the west by *Dead-man's Bay.*

Nearer to us is the " Royal Watering-place " of the drama, its blue bay rounding before it (210). Through our glasses we can distinguish the esplanade, *Gloucester Lodge,* the king's residence—now the Gloucester Hotel—and near it the statue of the king. The Nothe protrudes into the bay, justifying its name.

Farther to the right we can get more glimpses of the Chesil Beach, which terminates at Abbotsbury—the *Abbotsea* of Wessex nomenclature—whose actual position is marked by St. Katharine's Chapel on the hill of the same name. *Pos'ham,* or Portisham, the home and birthplace of Captain Hardy, lies a trifle nearer to us. Then, looking up the Waddon Vale (the scene for the poem entitled " The Lacking

210.—WEYMOUTH FROM THE SEA.

211.—RAINBARROWS.

Sense "), we see the grim outline of *Black'on* with the Hardy Monument topping it—from which spot uprose the beacon flames which come before us in the next scene. Only the height of Ridgeway prevents us from looking on *Maidon*; but we can distinguish the notched outline of *Eggar-Dun*, far in the distance. *Pummery* lies right over *Durnover Great Field*, and close to it *Casterbridge*, due north. Here and there we can trace a small section of Long Ash Lane, but especially where it rises to *Higher Crowstairs Down*, on its way to *Ivell*.

Still carrying our gaze in the same direction we light on *Mellstock* Church, and the great house in *Knapwater Park*. The western portion of *Egdon Heath* becomes conspicuous, with Rainbarrows standing out strongly, backed by the *Yalbury Woods*; while under this lie the Froom-watered meadows, amid which we can just discern the roofs of *Blooms-End* and the *Quiet Woman Inn*. Bulbarrow is in the distance beyond, and far away rises the hill-town of *Shaston*. Still farther round, and we come upon the village of *Stickleford*; then Clyffe Clump and Bere Hill, and behind that *Greenhill*, where the fair is held, and behind that again the hills that shut out *Shottsford-Forum*. Right over *Wellbridge* we see the pottery chimney which is close to *Anglebury*, with a wide stretch of *Egdon Heath* between us and it; behind *Anglebury* is *Havenpool*, its harbour glittering in the sunlight; and away in the far distance is the shimmering green haze that marks the *Great Forest*.

Due east of us are the undulating Chaldon Downs, and beyond them we can see Nine-Barrow Down, where it dips to *Corvesgate Castle*. Preston Hill hides *Oxwell Hall* from us, also the village of *Nether-Moynton*; but Holworth stands out boldly, and from it we can trace the position of *Lulstead Cove*.

The fifth scene of the second act takes us to Rainbarrows (211). This is the spot which formed such an oft-recurring background in "The Return of the

Native," at the commencement of which story it was the site of a fire, just as it is now. On the top of the largest of these barrows—once a neolithic burial-place —many a fire has flamed up to celebrate various events, its first kindling having originated probably in a religious ceremony, or perhaps even in a sacrificial rite; and later to honour the dead who were buried under the tumulus. That particular fire called a bon-fire, which was ostensibly supposed to commemorate Gunpowder Plot, was doubtless a survival from pre-historic times, inaugurated at a date long anterior to that of Guy Fawkes. Another, more recent, reason for the lighting of a fire on some high hill or building may be found in its use as a form of signalling over long distances, and many of our highest elevations bear evidence of having played this part in the history of the country, for the remains of old beacon-towers and huts may still be distinguished. We may recall that the news of the fall of Troy was signalled by a fire, then called a courier-fire. The name beacon has passed sometimes to the hill itself; Dunkery Beacon (scene of " The Sacrilege"), the apex of Exmoor, and many others testify to this.

The " Rainbarrows" under notice, like many other ancient burial-mounds, have been opened by unskilful hands; the interiors have been flung about on all sides, leaving the centres as cup-shaped depressions. Close beside the barrows was an old Roman road, the altitude of the heathery ridgeway having doubtless been selected on account of the wide outlook which it commands. In our author's description of the spot we learn that a house of turves with a brick chimney stood on the sheltered side of the barrow during the wars with Napoleon, and evidence remaining is the foundation on which the brick chimney-shaft was reared. These bricks have been gradually dis-tributed far and wide, and have been lost in the growth of heather and bracken which clothes the tumulus and the extensive waste around it; but by diligent search we may still find some here and there.

We are told of the wide vista which extends before the gaze of any one standing on the summit of Rainbarrow in the following passage : " Something in the feel of the darkness and the personality of the spot imparts a sense of uninterrupted space around, the view by day extending from the cliffs of the Isle of Wight eastward to Blackdon Hill by Deadman's Bay westward, and south across the valley of the Froom to the ridge that screens the channel." If we climb to the top of Rainbarrow to-day we can, in a clear atmosphere, distinguish each of these points, excepting only the cliffs of the Isle of Wight, which are shut out from us by a growth of trees on a more distant part of *Egdon Heath.* Just as on Bincombe Down, so here we can identify many of those places which we have already examined at close quarters ; *Yalbury Wood* hides from us the hills which surround *Abbot's Cernel,* where the Cerne Giant is cut out on the grassy hill-side. To the eastward is *Kingsbere Hill*—the spot towards which one of the beacon-keepers was continually directing his gaze ; and just behind it rises above the tree-tops the tower of Charborough—the *Welland Tower* of " Two on a Tower." The tumuli which top Bincombe Down are easily distinguished ; and farther to the west we can trace the long straight white road leading up to the top of the Ridgeway, where we were standing in the first scene. Parts of *Casterbridge* are open to us, and to the eastward of the town we obtain a glimpse of the gables and chimneys of Max Gate—the residence of our author—the Max turnpike-road passing close beside it. Blackdon Hill and the Hardy Monument are also in sight.

Both there and on *Kingsbere Hill* (212) were stored ricks of dry fuel, ready to kindle when the signal was given, and we shall remember that the beacon-keepers were considerably agitated as to which spot they ought

212.—BLACK HILL, BERE REGIS.

213.—THE GIANT, CERNE ABBAS.

to watch for the signal. The advent of Mrs. Cantle
on the barrow led to the recital of some of the superstitions current regarding Napoleon : " They say that
he lives upon human flesh, and has rashers o' baby for
breakfast—for all the world like the Cernel Giant in
old ancient times!" Then as now the mystery con-
cerning the Giant of Cerne was profound ; in a previous
chapter we have touched on this matter (213). The
illuminating remark of Jem Purchess, " He's come!" is
followed by the immediate kindling of the Rainbarrow
beacon-fire, and this is still burning when morning
dawns and discloses many of the dwellers on the coast
hurrying inland—as in the traditional accounts.

Both the first scene of the fourth act and the seventh
scene of the fifth act are staged at Weymouth. In the
former we are introduced to "a room in the red brick
Royal residence known as Gloucester Lodge" (214).
A footnote tells us "this weather-beaten old building
though now an hotel is but little altered." The description of the various features visible from the windows of
the building is so comprehensive as to necessitate no
elaboration on the part of the present writer. A certain
window in the front of the house used to be pointed out
as being the one from which the king was wont to gaze
on the crowds that promenaded the esplanade or played
their old-time games on the yellow sands below. Here,
at his favourite summer resort, we find the king dis-
cussing matters of cogent state importance with Pitt,
and in the course of their meeting the king refers to
" Lord Nelson's captain—Hardy—whose old home
stands in the peaceful vale hard by us here." We
have already visited Captain Hardy in his home at
Portisham when in imagination we journeyed there
with Bob Loveday in the book entitled " The Trumpet-
Major " (215). We are further interested in "Nelson's
Hardy " by reason of his consanguinity with our author,
although the latter's immediate forebears were at that
time resident a long distance from Portisham.

The second time that Weymouth comes before us

214.—THE GLOUCESTER HOTEL, WEYMOUTH.

215.—CAPTAIN HARDY'S HOUSE, PORTISHAM.

as a background in the present book is when we over-hear a conversation between some of the boatmen and the burghers in an ancient hostel near the harbour, called the *Old Rooms Inn*. This inn is still discover-able, close to the quay on the other side of the harbour-bridge, with its Elizabethan details at the back ; but its front has been modernised to a large extent, and would probably be scarcely recognisable by its habitués of the early nineteenth century.

Our interest now centres in the scene on board the *Victory*, and it is with feelings of solemnity that we tread the self-same deck on which Nelson and Hardy paced. Lying at rest in Portsmouth Harbour, and anchored nearly midway between Portsea and Gosport, its old-world appearance is strongly intensified by con-trast with the modern battleships which may be seen almost alongside the old relic of Trafalgar (216). Near it is moored the *Alberta*—the boat in which Queen Victoria crossed to the Island, and the last boat on which she set foot — while just inside it rides the Royal Yacht. Thus the *Victory* is surrounded by honourable companions that have taken part in many a history-making episode.

We might well wish that the famous ship had not been tampered with, that this memorial to one of England's greatest men had been preserved to us intact, and without being subjected to modern utilisations. Its employment as a training-ship, however, has necessi-tated many alterations, and we see a somewhat ruthless disregard for the old in order to make room for the modern.

In making our way from the Hard to the ship we may either select a boat at haphazard, or inquire for one Samuel Munt, a direct descendant of one of Nelson's crew. Samuel's grandfather served on board the *Victory*, and, provided the old man is in the humour for yarning, he will tell us stories and details handed down to him by his grandfather, tales which seem to bridge time and to take us back to the very days when

216.—The "Victory."

217.—Shockerwick House.

the *Victory* was crowded with brave and eager men, who looked on their captain with a regard that almost amounted to reverence.

On board, we still seem to inhale the atmosphere surrounding Nelson and Hardy and their gallant men. On the main deck, close to the skylight of Nelson's cabin, is the brass tablet marking the spot where he fell.   There is Hardy's cabin, and within it the barge, presented by Queen Victoria, in which his body was conveyed from Greenwich to Whitehall on its way to St. Paul's for burial.   Many interesting prints, maps, and paintings are to be seen in the cabins, including a picture of the death-scene executed from a drawing made on the voyage home ; it is heavily framed in oak, which was once part of the ship.   The floor of the lower deck is the original one ; in the cockpit we are shown the table on which the wounded were laid out ready for the surgeons.

Here, we read in Act V. Part I. of the book before us, in this "low-beamed deck" were the wounded men, "some groaning, some silently dying, some dead." The cockpit is still lighted by dim lanterns, giving it a strange appearance of rehabilitation, and by the faint glimmer we see the pile of wreaths which are placed there annually on the 21st of October by Nelson's descendants, marking the place where he lay and conversed with Hardy, and where his final words were spoken.

The action now turns to London, then to Weymouth once more, and, for a short scene, to Shockerwick House.   We find this grand old house, surrounded by its picturesque scenery, about four miles from Bath. It was formerly the seat of the Wiltshire family, and the Picture Gallery forms the background against which Pitt and Wiltshire stand out in the sixth act of this Part (217).

Passing over all the intermediate Continental fields

218.—FORDINGTON VICARAGE.

219.—FORDINGTON CHURCH.

of action we come to that of *Durnover Green, Caster-bridge.* We were close beside its original (Fordington Green) when we were exploring the country of " The Mayor of Casterbridge." It is still an open space, but its environs have been encroached on and altered since the date when the bonfire was lighted and the effigy of Napoleon hanged on a rough gallows and burned. We are told that a huge crowd had assembled from all parts to witness the pageant. One man had come from *Stourcastle*—approximately Sturminster Newton—a distance of more than twenty miles, while many familiar faces are brought before us as we gaze in imagination at the throng. The old vicarage, against the garden door of which the vicar is represented to be leaning, is the ivy-shrouded house now standing opposite the new vicarage (218). As the flames rise up they illumine " the grey tower of Durnover church hard by " (219), and it requires little imagination to enable us to picture the scene, and even to think we hear the huzzas and shoutings of the excited crowd which is gathered round the fire. It may be mentioned that, according to the Oxford Dictionary, bonfire is probably a corruption of bonefire and originally signified a fire of bones. The burning of an effigy seems to be a relic of pagan sacrifices, when people were burnt alive in order to appease the wrath of the gods.

The entrance of the mail-coach, bearing the stirring news that Napoleon had been given up to public vengeance and that "anybody may take his life in any way, fair or foul," leads us to the end of the scene. The effigy is "blown to rags," for the flames have reached the powder ; the crowd disperses ; the band marches away playing "When War's Alarms " (an air of the date) ; and, to quote our author's words, " the fire goes out and darkness curtains the scene."

CHAPTER IV

"TIME'S LAUGHING-STOCKS"

THE REVISITATION

In this poem we can follow mentally in the tread of the restless sojourner as he passes under the gateway of the barracks at *Casterbridge* (220), and, descending the High Street, walks over the "battered bridge." We have many times followed this route, particularly when we were examining the surroundings in "The Mayor of Casterbridge," where this bridge—Grey's Bridge—also figured. Dorchester has of course altered very considerably since the 'forties, when Henchard was imagined as Mayor, but even to-day we may obtain some idea of *Old Casterbridge* if we view it at night, when folk are abed and asleep and our footsteps echo noisily on the worn flagstones of the High Street. Grey's Bridge, built 1748, teems with associations ; it frequently becomes the "Bridge of Sighs" in the Wessex Novels and Poems, for it has figured many times as the spot where those oppressed in spirit paused to contemplate the alternative to continued existence.

Crossing the bridge, the solitary man continues up the "lonely Lane of Slyre" towards Waterstone Ridge (221). This road, too, we have travelled, when we journeyed with Burthen in his carrier's van towards *Longpuddle*. But when we reach the apex of the long incline we leave the high road, to enter the "downland thinly

220.—THE BARRACKS, DORCHESTER.

221.—WATERSTONE RIDGE.

grassed," where we come upon the barrows—"immemorial funeral piles"—scattered here and there, some
showing their ancient shape, others wellnigh levelled
with the ground. If we search diligently we can find
a boundary-stone of some size, now half-buried and
overgrown, but undoubtedly deserving the title of
"sarsen." Where it originally came from we can
only conjecture—perhaps from the Wiltshire downs,
where the hill-sides and valleys are thick with them,
and where they have earned the name of "the grey
wethers" from their suggestive likeness to sheep
lying at rest.

The wayfarer's visitant lived "below there in the
Vale," and we may like to picture her residence as the
old farmstead called Muston, once a manor-house (222).
He wakes when the sun is rising, when it blazed
from "the Milton Woods to Dole-hill"—two prominences which rear themselves out of the vale to the
north-east and north, and which can be readily distinguished from this spot. And then in fancy we see
him retracing his steps, descending the hill, recrossing
the "battered bridge," and entering the gateway of
the barracks.

A TRAMPWOMAN'S TRAGEDY

If we will follow the tracks

> My fancy-man, and jeering John,
> And Mother Lee, and I

took on an eventful day, we shall need to climb some
of the greatest heights of western Wessex and dip
down into some of its lowest levels. Such a course
will bring before us scenery of exceeding beauty and
diversity.

The road which leads from Dorchester to Crewkerne passes through Maiden Newton and climbs
Whitesheet Hill. Leaving Crimmercrock Lane on
our right hand, and passing Benvill Lane on the top of
Toller Down (223), we soon reach Wynyard's Gap, some

222.—MANOR-HOUSE, MUSTON.

223.—BENVILL LANE.

224.—WYNYARD'S GAP INN.

225.—MARSHALL'S ELM.

three miles from Crewkerne (224). From here our road is practically due north ; we pass "sad Sedge-Moor," climb "the toilsome Poldon crest," and in due course reach Marshall's Elm, the scene of the imagined tragedy (225). This inn has now become a farm-house, its licence having dropped thirty or more years ago. It stands at the crest of the ridgeway, above the village of the same name, just at the junction of five roads. A wonderful view extends from this point, the moors lying below to the westward, and Glastonbury Tor rising out of the valley northwards. The old swinging sign, bearing a picture of the battle of Sedgemoor, has entirely disappeared, though it is still remembered by some of the older inhabitants.

For months previous the quartette had wandered here and there, in the *Great Forest*—the New Forest, once the chief haunt of gipsy-folk,—through "Blackmoor wide"—the Vale with which Hardy readers are very familiar as "the Vale of the Little Dairies," —crossing the Parret, climbing the Mendips, fording the Yeo—the stream that runs beside the town of Yeovil and gives its name thereto,—and thence through the Marshwood Fens.

Some of the "lone inns" visited are still in existence. King's Stag was burnt down about fifteen years ago, and its site is now filled by some modern cottages. Nearly opposite, at the pottery, we may see the post from which its sign depended, but the sign was blown down a short time back ; it is still preserved, however, and there is a proposition afoot to have it repaired and erected at the cross-roads close by. The sign depicts the head of a stag with a collar round its neck, and on it is the following doggerel :—

> When Julius Cæsar reigned here
> I was but then a little deer ;
> When Julius Cæsar reigned King
> Around my neck he put this ring.
> Whoever doth me overtake,
> Pray spare my life for Cæsar's sake.

King's Stag was once famous for its Maypole; the revels started on June 11 and lasted for three days, during which time people flocked from far and near, and the old inn overflowed with visitors to such an extent that many had to be refused accommodation.

Windwhistle Inn—another halting-place of the four characters in the tragedy—stands about four miles from Crewkerne on the road leading to Exeter (226). It was once a noted posting-house, and still preserves many of its old-time characteristics, including the high-backed settles in the kitchen. It was also famed as a favourite haunt of certain highwaymen; its isolated position no doubt made it an excellent rendezvous. Many stories are still told of the gang who met there. An old well—now foundered in—used to be pointed out as the hiding-place wherein the bodies of the victims were thrown.

"The Horse on Hintock Green" is discoverable in the White Horse at Middlemarsh—one of the villages that go to complete the *Hintocks* of "The Wood-landers" (227). It is a picturesque building of weather-worn brick; the tiled roof is laid to a pattern and the tiles themselves are moss-grown, the chimneys are massive and elaborated with dentil courses under the copings.

"The cozy house at Wynyard's Gap" aforesaid deserves that title to-day; it lies close to the road just after we begin the descent of the hill towards Crewkerne.

The "hut renowned on Bredy Knap" has long ceased to be an inn, though the fabric remains. It is easily discovered on the roadside between Dorchester and Bridport.

It was at *Ivel-chester*, the old name here used for Ilchester, that the hanging is supposed to take place. The gaol was built in 1188. The town's decadence was perceptibly helped by the introduction of railways, the line leaving Ilchester out of count; but until then it formed a good centre for agricultural trading, situated

226.—WINDWHISTLE INN.

227.—THE WHITE HORSE INN, MIDDLEMARSH

as it is on the margin of the moors, where vast herds of cattle graze. Its market dates from before the Conquest. The river Yeo or Ivel runs close beside the town, and right on its bank stood the said county gaol. We may still see the hanging-chamber with its balcony, from which the victim was launched forth to swing over the river (228). Not far from the thriving town of Yeovil, Ilchester is a sleepy, old-world place, saturated with a feeling of restfulness which is not lost on the stranger who visits it. A picturesque cross stands in the market-place, erected to ensure fair dealing between buyer and vendor, and just behind it is the hall wherein numberless prisoners were tried and condemned. Away from the town stretch the wide moors, extending westwards to the Bristol Channel.

Glastonbury, or Glaston Twelve Hides, which also comes into this poem, is a town of absorbing interest to the archæologist ; its Tor, once an island, but now a peninsula hemmed in on three sides by the river Brue, is visible from many miles distant (229). We must not pause to examine the town in detail, but a few of its main features may be enumerated. The abbot's kitchen—practically all that remains of the domestic part of the once famous abbey—is a curious and unique building ; outside the walls are square, the inside is octagonal, and the corners are filled in with fireplaces and chimneys. The Chapel of St. Joseph is transitional work of the twelfth century. The Great Church, the longest in the whole country, measured 410 feet from east to west, and was 80 feet in width in the nave. The Glastonbury Thorn is supposed to have been planted by Joseph of Arimathea, who, on his arrival, stuck his staff into the ground ; it took root and grew, and is said to be a distinct variety, flowering twice a year.

Many and interesting are the legends associated with Glastonbury, one of the most curious being that Joseph of Arimathea, the leader of twelve apostles

228.—THE HANGING-CHAMBER, ILCHESTER GAOL.

229.—GLASTONBURY TOR.

sent from Gaul by St. Philip, erected the first church
here, a small wattled building. From early times,
and through the Middle Ages, it was the scene of
many pilgrimages.

A Sunday Morning Tragedy

This poem depends for its background on *Pydel
Vale*, a locality which figures in "Crusted Characters,"
where the adjoining villages of Pydelhinton and
Pydeltrenthide are known to us under the joint name
of *Longpuddle*. It was in the church of the former of
these parishes that the banns were called, in circumstances reputed to be veracious (230).

Bereft

The *Casterbridge* features here brought to our
notice have already been examined. *Durnover Lea*
is more or less akin to Fordington Moor; while
Grey's Bridge has been identified many times.

The Curate's Kindness

It was at *Pummery*, or else at *Ten-hatches Weir*,
that the misogynist of this ironical poem thought to
end his forty years of matrimonial infelicity. *Pummery*,
or Poundbury, weir is a deep dark silent pool in fair
weather, and a raging torrent after rain (231). It lies
snugly under the escarpments of Poundbury Camp and
is reached most easily from the Sherborne road out of
Dorchester. Ten-hatches is the weir in the Froom
meadows, in sight of Grey's Bridge, and is familiar to
us as the hole wherein Henchard, in "The Mayor
of Casterbridge," is imagined to have watched his
effigy floating on the morning following the skimmity
ride (232).

The Voice of the Thorn

Doubtless this poem might have been suggested
by any thorn on any down, but familiarity with our

230.—PYDELHINTON.

231.—POUNDBURY WEIR, DORCHESTER.

author's methods leads us to suppose that a particular thorn tree was before him as he wrote. This was in fact the case. From Upper Bockhampton there is a footpath leading across Kingston Park to Stinsford Church, and here we can see old thorn trees, many of which strike us as reasonably typical.

AFTER THE CLUB DANCE

" Black'on frowns east on Maidon." *Black'on* is a local pronunciation of Blackdown, the heathery upland from which the Hardy Monument rears itself (233). A climb to the top of the Monument will reward us with a magnificent outlook : the Needles on one hand ; the Devonshire coast on the other ; and all the intervening country, exhibiting to the eye many of the backgrounds to the Wessex Novels and Poems. Around us in the distance and mid-distance are several eminences where beacon fires blazed at the time when the landing of Napoleon was expected, as in " The Dynasts" ; we look down on Maidon Castle and can follow each ridge and ditch. Retracing our steps to Dorchester, we pass close beside that ancient earthwork, which, according to recent research, appears to have been the achievement of three distinct epochs of history. And if we turn our gaze back after another mile or two, and it happens to be near the setting hour of the sun, we shall then obtain a true impression of the fact that " Black'on frowns east on Maidon " still, just as it did in the days when *Maidon* was the *Dunium* of Ptolemy.

A WIFE WAITS

The " Club-room " mentioned here has been swept away. It stood once facing on to North Square, better known to Hardy readers as *Bull-stake Square*, in which guise it comes before us repeatedly in " The Mayor of Casterbridge." We read in a footnote that

232.—TEN HATCHES WEIR, DORCHESTER.

233.—HARDY MONUMENT ON BLACKDOWN.

" The Bow (where the wife waited) . . . is not now so described," but, thanks to the present Curator of the County Museum, the old name has been replaced.

AFTER THE FAIR

We are still in the vortex of the Dorchester of olden times. *Cornmarket Place*, *The Cross*, *The White Hart*, *Grey's Bridge*, and the *High Street*— all these we have already explored ; *Clock-corner steps* is the only feature foreign to us, and this spot has been altered too completely to allow us to trace any points of similarity between it and the steps which now lead into the Corn Exchange.

THE HOME-COMING

The scenery here is peculiarly appropriate to the theme of the poem. Toller Down was chosen by our author with due regard to effect. It is a lonesome spot, quite sufficient in itself to explain the utter feeling of isolation which gripped the bride on her introduction to the wind-swept upland (234). Coming thither from *Ivel* (*i.e.* Yeovil) the contrast is further impressed. If we visit Toller Down in the autumn or winter we shall have little difficulty in proving to ourselves the truth contained in our author's description of the spot. The boisterous wind, howling, driving before it everything movable, cutting like a knife over the ridges, forming a concentrated draught through the valleys and cuttings, hurries away down "Crimmercrock's long lane"—the road leading from Maiden Newton to Rampisham—still so called.

A CHURCH ROMANCE

The church of Stinsford would seem to serve for the background of this sonnet-scene, but before the West Gallery and high pews were removed. It will

234.—Cottage on Toller Down.

235.—Puddletown Church.

be remembered that the music here was performed by
a string choir—just as we read of it in " Under the
Greenwood Tree."

The Christening

As we explore the old church of Puddletown we
cannot help noticing the worn "gallery stairs." Until
about the year 1840 the music, here as at Stinsford,
was produced by a string choir (235). In "the woods
afar" we let our thoughts turn to Yellowham Woods,
another feature in the book just mentioned.

The Dead Quire

This takes us again into the *Mellstock* country and
to the church of Stinsford. The "dormered inn" is no
longer the licensed house of former years, but we may
trace its likeness in the thatch-roofed dwelling close to
the bridge at Lower Bockhampton (236). Passing
through the " Bank-walk wicket," a pathway leads us
beside the margin of the "crystal Froom" (237-238);
we leave it to mount the rise called "Church-way"
(239) ("Church Lane" elsewhere), and after passing
the church we continue an upward path, called here
" Moaning Hill" by our author, the name coming
doubtless from the weird sound made by the wind as
it passes among the twigs and branches of the clump
of chestnut trees just in front. The " Mead of
Memories" is, of course, represented by the watered
ground below the church.

By the Barrows

There is a small group of barrows on the heath
adjacent to Upper Bockhampton called Rainbarrows,
inevitably associated in our minds with "The Dynasts"
and "The Return of the Native," but although we
recognise and identify these jutting prominences we

236.—COTTAGE, ONCE AN INN, LOWER BOCKHAMPTON.

237.—THE PATH BESIDE THE RIVER, LOWER BOCKHAMPTON

310

238.—THE FROOM NEAR BOCKHAMPTON.

239.—CHURCH LANE, STINSFORD.

must not be too literal as regards their position, for it is evident from the descriptions of their environment that in our author's mind they are imagined as standing in a more central portion of the *Egdon* waste. This is so in the poem entitled

THE ROMAN ROAD,

where the line "as the pale parting-line in hair" brings vividly back to us the early chapters of "The Return of the Native," where the same simile is employed. Evidences of this old road are but faintly discernible on the western side of *Egdon Heath*, but when we trace it farther eastward—as for instance in the neighbourhood of Wimborne—it betrays itself as a much more clearly marked *via* and approximates closely to the description.

THE VAMPIRINE FAIR

Wingreen Hill is near Salisbury; the *Manor Court* can hardly be other than a fictitious presentment of Rushmore House; and in *Shastonb'ry* we easily recognise Shaftesbury.

THE PINE PLANTERS

Here is the country of "The Woodlanders" before us once more. No particular spot is mentioned, but such detail seems scarcely necessary. We have thoroughly explored this country and the *Hintock* villages and hamlets, and the poem interests us more as a reminder of the book in question than as one which breaks fresh ground for topographical research.

THE DEAR

"Fairmile Hill-top" is the summit of the hill on the old Sherborne Road from Dorchester, and from it we obtain a wonderful outlook over the southern landscapes. It is said to derive its name from being a fair or full mile long.

THE NOBLE LADY'S TALE

Stinsford again forms a background, and in the church we come upon the "yellowing marble" with

240.—CLYFFE CLUMP.

the pair of linked hearts, which forms the Monument spoken of in the poem.

YELL'HAM WOOD'S STORY

"Coomb-Firtrees" stand on a slight eminence just outside the Coomb—a grassy eweleaze close to

Puddletown and on the margin of *Egdon Heath.*
"Clyffe-hill Clump" is a high, wind-swept, fir-crowned
hill standing on the ridge which separates the valleys
of the Froom and Pydel, and recognisable as a familiar
landmark from long distances (240). Just below is the
little hamlet of Clyffe. "Yell'ham Wood" scarcely
needs further elucidation, for it has already come
before us frequently in our explorations.

INDEX

(Real names in Roman type ; fictitious names in Italics)

INDEX

THE WESSEX OF THOMAS HARDY

THE END

ACHEVÉ D'IMPRIMER
SUR LES PRESSES OFFSET
DE L'IMPRIMERIE REDA S.A.,
A CHÊNE-BOURG (GENÈVE), SUISSE.

MARS 1969